Samed

Journal of a West Bank Palestinian

Raja Shehadeh

Adama Books
NEW YORK

Copyright © 1984 by Raja Shehadeh and Adama Books
All rights reserved

Originally published in Israel under the title *The Third Way* by Adam Publishers, Jerusalem.

No part of this publication may be reproduced, stored in a retrieval system, or transmitted in any form or by any means, electronic, mechanical, photocopying, recording, or otherwise (brief quotations used in magazines or newspaper reviews excepted), without the prior permission of the publisher.

Printed in the United States of America

Library of Congress Cataloging in Publication Data
Shehadeh, Raja.
   Samed: Journal of a West Bank Palestinian.

   1. Shehadeh, Raja. 2. Palestinian Arabs—West Bank—
Biography. 3. West Bank—Politics and government.
4. Jewish-Arab relations—1973-   . I. Title.
DS119.7.S4673   1984   956.95′1   [B]   83-25647
ISBN 0-915361-02-7 (pbk.)

Adama Books, 306 West 38 Street, New York, New York 10018

Contents

Preface	vii

Winter, 1979–80
Occupational Problems	3
Is Johnny Sāmid?	4
Jericho in Winter	7
Where Are the Judges?	11
It Can Only Be a Dream	16
The Green Kufiyeh	20
Khalil	23
Colonized	27
Sāmid for How Long?	30
Enoch	34

Spring 1980 Journal
	43

Summer, 1980
Fear	61
The Gentle Ones	65
The Shooting of Hani	67
Maha	74
Kamil, Another Sāmid	77
The Grave	80
Pornography	84

The Visit	89
The World Is Like a Wheel, Like a Cucumber	95
The Wheel	96

Autumn 1980 Journal   101

Faces, 1980   133

Epilogue, January 1982   141

Preface

*Sāmid** means 'the steadfast', 'the persevering'. It is the name coined during the 1978 Baghdad Conference for the one and a half million Palestinians living under Israeli occupation. It was then that Arab politicians outside officially acknowledged the urgency of stemming the mass exile of Palestinians from the occupied territories† and of trying to halt the Israeli government's expropriation of huge tracts of land on the West Bank. We, who had been living under occupation for ten years, were now called on to be *samidīn* and urged to adopt the stance of *sumūd*: to stay put, to cling to our homes and land by all means available. A special pan-Arab fund, *Amwal es-sumūd*, was set up to help us combat the collapse of our social and economic fabric, caused by the Israeli colonization of our land.

This official recognition, and the funds, were welcome, if somewhat belated. It was not news to us that Israel was pursuing a policy of driving us into exile – either by overt banishment or by making our life here progressively unbearable. For years before anyone acknowledged it, we had found ourselves systematically deprived of basic human rights and had watched our land being closed off to us and handed over to Israeli settlers.

* This is the masculine form. The feminine form is *Sāmdeh* and the plural *samidīn*. The state of perseverance, hanging on, is *sumūd*.
† During the 1967 War, an estimated 100,000 went into exile. The number of Palestinians who have gone into exile since the occupation began is estimated at 150,000–180,000.

vii

Long before Arab politicians outside defined *sumūd* as a pan-Arab objective it had been practised by every man, woman and child here struggling on his or her own to learn to cope with, and resist, the pressures of living as a member of a conquered people. *Sumūd* is watching your home turned into a prison. You, *Sāmid*, choose to stay in that prison, because it is your home, and because you fear that if you leave, your jailer will not allow you to return. Living like this, you must constantly resist the twin temptations of either acquiescing in the jailer's plan in numb despair, or becoming crazed by consuming hatred for your jailer and yourself, the prisoner. It is from this personal basis that *sumūd* for us, in contrast with politicians outside, is developing from an all-encompassing form of life into a form of resistance that unites the Palestinians living under Israeli occupation.

One of the greatest threats to our *sumūd* is the feeling of isolation. The Palestinians' political activities and demands are well known and reported. But we *samidīn* are silent about the actual day-to-day experience of living under occupation. It is not only military orders and the threat of banishment that make us keep our thoughts and feelings to ourselves. Our struggle for survival is totally consuming. It was to break out of this silence that I began writing about my life and the lives of other *samidīn*. This book is a selection of stories and journal entries written during 1980. In retrospect, I can see that this year was a crucial test for my *sumūd*. Although my life is in various ways much easier than that of many other *samidīn*, I think we have enough in common for the pieces collected here to give a sense of what *sumūd* is.

I am fully aware of the risk I am taking in publishing what I have written. But many other Palestinians and some Israelis are also taking risks. It is my hope that more and more of us will stand up, each in his or her own way, against the inhumanity of the policies now being pursued by the Israeli government.

Many people have taken part in the making of this book – by telling me their stories, by reading and commenting on the various drafts, and by going over the final manuscript. To protect people appearing in the stories, I have changed all names except for those publicly known. I wish to express my gratitude to all of them. I have also changed a few dates slightly to avoid people being identified.

I wish here to thank my mother, Widad Shehadeh (whose name means 'love'), from whose natural talent for storytelling and humour I have learnt a lot, and also my father Aziz ('the dear one') Shehadeh, who guided me through the first difficult years of professional life under occupation and made it possible for me to write.

Warm thanks are due to my friends Charles Shammas, Lisa Taraki and Henry Abramovitch for their valuable suggestions; Yehuda Melzer of Adam Publishers, Jerusalem, for encouraging me to prepare this book for publication; and Rosheen Eilan and Michael Eilan for their interest and technical assistance. Particular thanks go to Jonathan Kuttab, my companion through many years and projects, whose influence pervades these pages.

Finally, a very special acknowledgement is due to Naomi Eilan for her dedication, deep personal commitment and editorial skills which helped give shape to this book.

Raja Shehadeh
Ramallah, West Bank
1982

Samed

Winter, 1980

Occupational Problems

My problem with newspapers is that I can't settle on the right time to read them. In the morning they darken the day, at noon they kill my appetite, after lunch they make me sick, and in the evening they set the pattern of my nightmares.

So I don't read the papers every day. Today I did. Scanning the headlines I find that Begin wants to enforce Israeli law on the West Bank, that Agriculture Minister Sharon plans to surround Nablus with a band of Jewish settlements, and that Sharon has leased fifty dunums* of land from the Israeli Lands Administration, and has employed Palestinian shepherds to tend his own flocks on it. Nice twist, that.

Also: a resident of the Jewish urban West Bank settlement, Kiryat Arba, has been stabbed to death in nearby Hebron. His name has not yet been published. He is a new immigrant and his parents abroad have not yet been notified. The Jewish settlers are calling for revenge. Ministers and army generals have come to Kiryat Arba to calm the population.

I don't need the newspapers to find out what happens next. Tribal sagas follow a predictable pattern. The young man must have come here, perhaps from Europe, fired by the stories of the Zionist salvation of the Jewish people in the Land of Greater Israel. They omitted to tell him that another tribe already lived on this land. Dazzled by the prospect of fulfilling his vision, he settles in the middle of an area densely

---

*A dunum is a measurement of area, equal to 1,000 square metres or just under a quarter of an acre.

populated by the native tribe, and is blind to its existence.

One day, a member of the tribe that was pushed aside to let this young man's dreams flourish makes his presence felt by stabbing him to death. The Jews well up in anger and revenge is sought: kill the Arabs, wipe them out, show the world who owns this land. But their elders, their wise elders, come to their settlement to appease them. They say: do not worry. We shall teach the enemy that our blood is sacred. The land will be cleansed of their presence, but do not act foolishly. Trust us. Wait until the world isn't watching. We have the power and the means to make those Arabs *want* to leave. But wait until no one is watching.

And the daily little instalments in the newspapers show us that the angry Jews should trust their elders. They are right. The world will not watch the slow strangulation of my people. Even I cannot face the newspapers every day.

Is Johnny Sāmid?

I can now tell by looking at people in the street who amongst them is of the samidīn.

The women, the girls: the free-moving body, the proud, carefree gaze and the open laugh betray the Beirut girl. She cannot be from here. The Arab girl from Haifa is also different. She is less inhibited than the Sāmdeh, but there is something strained in her manner compared with her Beirut sister. It is as though her carefree manner is an attitude adopted in defiance rather than her right by birth.

As to the men – I sometimes think that I can tell where they come from by the degree of defeat in their eyes. Those from the pre-'67 Israel seem to have a more deathlike gaze than their brothers from Arab countries. And I have watched our faces, the faces of the samidīn, gradually assume the lines on the faces of our brothers in Israel since 1948 – Arabs who look as if they have long forgotten their natural right to be their own masters.

Or so it seems. But then Johnny's face bounces into mind – bright-eyed, laughing, gentle. Is he Sāmid? On the face of it, no. When Johnny returned from several years of study in the States, he was inclined to say things that would definitely reveal him as new to the art of sumūd. I remember once when we saw a girl limping in the street, he was shocked to hear that she had been shot by soldiers during a demonstration. 'I cannot believe they shot at her. In my mind, the people shot at are in faraway places, fedayeen who are tracked down in remote hills and caves,' said Johnny.

That was not long after he came back, and he has of course learnt much since then. He went to the States to study when he was too young to take in the reality of sumūd – we were all too young, as was the occupation itself. Johnny has come back with the avowed objective of being Sāmid. More than a year has gone by and he remains hopeful, enthusiastic, full of plans to develop the West Bank economy, to promote cooperatives, to organize labour, to give content to the nationalistic role of the samidīn. He is constantly on the look-out for converts, candidates for his schemes and for ways of implementing them. He has an extraordinary capacity for work, and has already done more in the short time he has been here than many have ever dreamed of doing during the past thirteen years.

Some think he is childish. Some say that it is only a matter of time before his enthusiasm dies a natural death. Some are wary of his motives – they suspect him of spying, serving some foreign agency. The most revolutionary here say he was sent to fill us with hope within the existing framework, thus delaying that inevitable state of total frustration when the revolution, the uprising of the desperate masses, will begin.

But all the suspicions he arouses and the gossip that reaches his ears leave the spirits untouched. I have seen him using all his powers of persuasion, talking his heart out, trying to convince others to join him. And I have seen the suspicion in their eyes, and have heard them reason how his plans are bound to fail: 'The military authorities will stop you, the people here will not let you, little do you know, you have not been around long enough, you are idealistic, naïve.'

But Johnny is not defeated. True, his face looked uncharacteristically sad as he explained to me why he thought a general paralysis has gripped the West Bank, why so many people here have turned into machines. He explains this as an inevitable result of colonization, but he does not despair. As always, he ends on a cheerful note, with a new scheme, bound to succeed, for defeating the defeat.

So far, the military forces of occupation have left him alone. They will continue to do so for as long as they think that no one is listening to him and that his projects are falling flat. But when they come to suspect that he is being effective and is interfering with their plans, they will begin to pursue him, for he is not one of the league they have set up in our midst to carry out their designs.

They will begin to keep him under surveillance. He will be called for a visit to the military governor. They will keep him waiting for half a day until an 'expert' with a frightening face interrogates him. First, they will let him see how much they know about him. Then he will be asked to give a detailed account of his activities. Sometimes this alone is enough to squelch a person. But if they do not succeed in frightening him, they will begin calling him to headquarters again and again, each time to another department, a different interrogation room, varying their tactics until they discover which method works best. They may even instruct their agents to spread rumours to make him lose his credibility. They won't give him the permits he needs to get any of his projects started. And then, people won't have anything more to do with him, because no project associated with him will get off the ground if he is out of favour with the authorities. But if he persists and is perceived as a real danger, something will be found against him, and he will be taken in. No one will be able to prove what happened to him inside, but everyone will see how much weight he has lost and how subdued and defeated he looks when he is released. And if he revives after this and takes up where he left off, they will come one night, drive him to the border in a jeep, and the number of deportees will be increased by one.

Johnny is no fool. He knows all of this. So far he has been left alone. But if they begin, how long will he keep his smile, how long will he remain the irrepressible Johnny we love?

Jericho in Winter

My cousin from Amman came to visit me for my birthday. He was cursing for two whole days after he arrived, blaming me for everything he had gone through on the Allenby Bridge when crossing over from Jordan. The screams of the children as they were undressed to be searched; the sight of a corpse that was being transported for burial in the West Bank and was taken out of its coffin for a security check; the smell of the travellers' feet after hours of waiting for their shoes to be returned after being X-rayed; the heartrending wails of the mother whose fourteen-year-old son had been taken for interrogation and had not yet returned. . . All of this and the hours of waiting for one's name to be called.

'And I will never forget the old woman I was sitting next to,' he'd go on. 'Even after hearing the babies howling, the mourners wailing over the corpse, the mother sobbing for her child, she did not lose her good humour. As the names were called out she said she felt as if she was at a graduation ceremony. When my turn came, after seven hours, she said: "Congratulations, go and receive your certificate." And then, when her own name was called out, the Israeli officer said she was too slow in answering and made her wait until all 300 names were called. And still she smiled.

'And what the hell did I come here for anyway?' he'd end his monologue. 'Why did you drag me to this drab place, what is there here for anyone? Why don't you come to Amman – I'd give you the time of your life. We have cinemas, foreign restaurants, night clubs.'

Again and again he'd ask me why I never visit him, and I would answer: 'I don't go to Amman.' He did not, and would not, understand why. How could I tell him that seeing Palestinians in the Jordanian capital, men who have grown rich and now pay only wildly patriotic lip-service to our struggle, was more than my sumūd in my poor and beloved land could stomach?

Today, my birthday, I took my cousin to Jericho, which is the best place to go in the winter. He rented a big American car; with his Jordanian dinars (which we have begun to covet because of Israeli inflation) he could afford it. We drove down the winding roads, descending the lunar hills in circles till we reached the road sign that says SEA LEVEL. And then, from a turning in the road, we saw the pastel shades of the Dead Sea.

As we rode down I was thinking to myself how blessed we have been with the rains this year. Jericho, the driest of West Bank towns, is green again. Even Auja is lush. All the crops had died and the trees had withered when Jewish settlers dug artesian wells nearby, diverting the waters of the Auja spring. But now Auja is flourishing again: it is *sanat kheyr* (prosperous year). Nature seems to have intervened to delay our occupiers' strategy of making the farmers leave 'of their own free will'. With water we can last much longer, for ever. Perhaps God is changing sides.

The thought was killed by my cousin, who read out in scathing tones the road sign that has been set up at the entrance to Jericho, in English and in Hebrew – not in Arabic: WELCOME TO TAMAR REGIONAL COUNCIL.

'Is that where we're going? I had supposed in my innocence that we were driving to Ariha [the Arab name for Jericho]. I bet next thing you know, you will wake up to find that you too have been allotted a Hebrew name with 2,000-year-old credentials!' my cousin said.

I was silent. Ahead of us, we saw several parked station wagons. A few bearded men in black, heavy overcoats, sweating profusely in the heat of the day, were digging holes for poles and taking measurements. Scurrying back and forth was an American-looking blond man, his big belly bulging over his trousers.

'So, a new Jewish settlement in the making!' sneered my cousin. 'Why don't you do anything about them – don't you have any pride?'

Again I did not answer. I hated the accusing way he hurled his questions at me. I was worried about his reaction when we reached the military road-block. But I had prepared him for it, and we both held our breath and passed it without incident.

'Now we can think of the day ahead of us and just enjoy ourselves,' I said, rather like a mother trying to cajole her husband into overlooking their children's naughtiness. Why could he not see that he, and all the others who left, are as much to blame as we samidīn for the way things are here?

We entered the oasis of Jericho with a thump. I explained that the municipality had dug up the streets two months ago to install water-pipes, and had not yet re-paved the roads.

'What do they do with the *Amwal es-sumūd* we send them from Amman, eh?' He was referring to the money sent to the West Bank from Arabs outside, which supplies about sixty per cent of the municipalities' minuscule budget.

Again I did not attempt to answer. Whose fault is it that our towns are badly run? With all the obstacles, real and imagined, that the Israeli authorities place before a municipality, it is impossible to lay the blame squarely on anyone's shoulders.

As we drove into the centre of town, I saw my cousin's good spirits returning. He had been taunting me without much thought. He is an outsider by now, and nothing really hurts him as it does me. And I was glad to be swept up in his holidaymaker's view of the place: Jericho, beautiful, lazy Jericho, somehow calls for it. We drove fast, zig-zagging around people promenading on Jericho's wide main street. There are always people out in the streets, strolling slowly, or on bicycles. This tropical town seems to thumb its nose at everything, unimpressed and outwardly unscathed by the grimness of the occupation.

We drove through Parks Street, lined by citrus trees with fruit-laden branches sweeping down to the ground. Between the pavement and the street, water gurgled in the open irrigation channels, glimmering through the algae.

We zoomed on, Greek music blaring from the car. Heads turned to watch us. A girl wearing tight, scarlet trousers walked past us with her friends. She caught my eye and smiled and I laughed aloud with joy. She had the beautiful face of a fifteen-year-old, with the glowing, dark skin, curly hair and wide sensual mouth of Jericho girls.

I was glad to hear some words of praise from my cousin who confessed: 'Even in Amman we don't have such beautiful girls parading in the streets as that!'

A young man cycled past the girls. He swivelled his head to look at them, winking and pulling faces. An old woman with braided hair, wearing an exquisite black dress embroidered in red, grabbed at his handlebars to stop him colliding with her. The young man turned his head and his face froze in horror as he encountered the stern, hard-featured face of the Nawariyya – a gypsy tribe that is renowned for its tough women.

My cousin laughed, and with one perfect movement spun the wheel around and drove back along Parks Street. 'Look!' He pointed to a sign. 'There's the Abbolo Café. Why on earth must they write in English when they can't tell the difference between "p" and "b"?'

But I was only half listening. I suddenly realized why the

fable of the *Sleeping Beauty* had been on my mind since entering Jericho. There is a drugged, eerie undertone to the relaxed pace of this elegant town – as if a spell of unnatural slumber had been cast over it. The gracious villas, that used to belong to Palestinians who are called 'absentees', are now smothered in heavy, untended greenery. The overgrown tropical trees are beautiful, but somehow repulsive, and lend an unreal, almost sinister feeling to the gardens and streets. One of the villas has been taken over by an Israeli woman chemist who is trying to make shampoo out of young papayas. She buys as much fruit as she can lay her hands on. Many small farmers have begun planting only papaya to supply her with material for her experiments.

'Let's stop to eat hummus,' I said to my cousin, to cut short my thoughts. I wanted to recapture my earlier, easy joy. But the owner of the café we chose launched, uninvited, into a long account of why business has been so bad since the occupation. Inflation has reduced sales to locals, and the Israelis have cornered the tourist market . . . I didn't have the strength to stop him. And I thought: why should I try to protect my cousin from what goes on here? I had lost the fleeting, heady taste of what I was like, years ago, before the occupation had begun.

Where Are the Judges?

Sabha told me today about her day in court, where she went at the appointed hour to give evidence in a property claim against her neighbour. I myself see the civilian, Arab-staffed courts on the West Bank through the eyes of a lawyer. My worries are professional: the courts have been divested of their independence and power, and their standards have plummeted since the occupation began. But these preoccupations shield me from the role that the lawyers themselves and the judges play in the nightmare of someone who comes, unprotected, to our halls to seek justice. With Sabha I have lived through the horror. Here is her story.

I arrived at the court at nine o'clock. At the door I saw the one-eyed cleaning woman. She greeted me warmly and enthusiastically, with her seeing eye sparkling – she lives not far from me.

There was a lot of commotion: lawyers with dark suits pacing back and forth conspiring with clients; old men sitting hunched on the benches lining the hall; many old women squatting on the floor. I walked through the crowds to the courtroom and was beginning to get the feeling of awe that courts always produce in me.

No usher guarded the door. I slid it open and entered. The courtroom was empty. Three long black chairs were lined up behind the bar, empty. There were no judges.

I returned to the hall and asked people where the judges were, but they were all too busy and no one would answer me. I looked around me and saw doors leading to other rooms and thought, maybe someone there will know.

I entered the first one, opposite the courtroom. There were two desks with a clerk sitting behind each. I stood in the centre of the room.

'Do you want the Execution Officer or the Notary Public? I am the Notary Public,' the one sitting at the desk to my left said.

I didn't answer.

'Let's see your papers,' the same man said, holding out his hand.

'Who are the judges?' I asked.

He lost interest and dropped his hand; the Execution Officer, who was following the conversation, returned to his writing.

'They are not here,' the Notary Public said briefly and firmly. Though he did not say anything else, or make any motion, I felt an invisible hand ushering me out, and I succumbed.

Once again I was in the hall. The cleaning woman had taken up her brush and was sweeping the floor. She noticed me and smiled a sort of knowing, seductive smile and went on sweeping the cigarette butts and dirt. I decided to find a seat in the corner and wait.

Time was passing. More people were coming into the hall and the cigarette smoke was clouding the air, choking me. But none of the people here looked like the judge, and I had carefully been keeping tabs on everyone coming in. It was ten o'clock already.

'Ustāz* Ahmad es-Sayyid . . . Ustāz Sami Sam'an . . . Ustāz Subhi el-Khūri . . .' the usher was calling, and his shouts echoed through the building. He is calling the lawyers, I thought. The judges must have arrived.

The better-dressed amongst the crowd pushed their way through, carrying executive briefcases. They marched out proudly, heads held high. The old women squatting below craned their necks to look up, and were full of admiration; and the men sitting on the benches suspended their conversations and followed this short parade of well-trimmed gentlemen with their eyes, until it disappeared into the courtroom.

With the departure of the lawyers, we were left alone. The atmosphere became more solemn. There were no longer entourages surrounding the lawyers, circling in the hall, conspiring and puffing clouds of smoke. It was like this for the next fifteen minutes. No more cries could be heard from the usher. Only the occasional whispering of the crowds and the sound of my own breathing. Why not go into the courtroom, I thought to myself, and confront the judges and let them know I am here?

*Arabic for 'Mister'.

When I opened the courtroom door, I was struck by the stench of onions. They also had hummus and beans, and green peppers on the tray. Some were dipping their fingers to wipe what remained from the plates, others sat on the benches around the bar where the tray was placed, sipping their tea from glasses and smoking. I felt embarrassed to have intruded on their private party. There were no judges amongst these lawyers. I slipped out.

An old man leaning on his cane met me as I left the courtroom.

'Where are the judges?' I asked him.

'There are no judges,' he said. 'The real judges went away after the occupation. There are no judges now. No judges.'

I walked away from this old man. The tone of impending doom in his voice made me feel uneasy and I did not want to encourage him to tell me any more.

I walked into a room I had not entered before. Maybe the clerk here would know something.

'I told you a hundred times already I will not accept your papers. You have come too late!' the clerk was shouting at an old woman standing behind the counter.

'But I was served with these papers only last night.'

'I don't care. According to my records, the period allowed by the law has elapsed.'

'How could it have elapsed if I received them last night? Is the period allowed by the law for answering a case less than twenty-four hours?'

'Listen, lady, I'm busy. I can't speak to you all day. You know the way. Go out, out!' The clerk turned his back on her and faced the window.

The woman's head drooped. Slowly, she picked up her papers and her purse and moved away, out of the office into the hall, and then out of the court of law. The clerk followed her with his eyes, then got up and strolled out into the hall where he began chatting with some men.

I was left alone in his office. I saw that the windows had

wire netting and that the glass was thick with dirt. Papers and files, seals and stamps covered his desk. I would not find any assistance here. I walked out.

Many people stood up, and those with suits half bowed when a man in a silk suit entered the hall. Is he a judge, I wondered.

He did not return the greetings but darted glances out of the corners of his eyes, as though he were making a secret note of the atmosphere and the people present. Then he turned left, climbed up a few stairs and disappeared into a corridor.

'He's the secretary of the Israeli army officer in charge of the judiciary,' someone standing close by me whispered to his friend. 'He is the Israelis' man in court. Every day he sends them his report on what goes on here. The Israelis are happy with him, and he is happy. All his children are studying in England and America. He is better off than he ever was before.'

'Who's that man with the gun?' asked the companion of the knowledgeable man.

'He's Shahin Khadir. A criminal who was sentenced to life, and released soon after by the Israelis and given a gun. Lower your voice when you see him around.'

I was beginning to feel dizzy, and I needed fresh air. As I was walking out, the clerk followed me and asked me for the time. I told him it was eleven o'clock.

'*Maqtu'a! Ana maqtu'a!* [I am alone!]' an old woman near the entrance was wailing, slapping her left cheek with her right hand and her right cheek with her left. '*Wallah maqtu'a! Wallah maqtu'a!*' she repeated.

I asked her what was the matter.

'My neighbours, *hal 'arsat* [those bastards], beat me up every day. They want to take my house. They want to throw me out in the street. I have no one to turn to. *Maqtu'a ana, wallah maqtu'a.* My sons are away and my husband is dead.'

'Did you complain to the police?' I asked her.

'I did. Three times – and every time they say the judge must hear my case first before they can do anything. Who will I turn to? Who will protect me? They beat me up every night. Look, look at the sores on my body. See this wound here on my arm. See these blue marks. I cannot keep them out. I have no man to protect me. They break in and beat me up – aah! The judges are not coming. Where are the judges?'

A thought crossed my mind and I asked the woman: 'Why don't you go to the *mukhtar* [village elder] and make a *sulha* [peace meeting] and solve this in the traditional way?'

She looked at me incredulously, studying my expression, and said to me, as if she were repeating the obvious: '*El haq qad ishabu* [Right is might].'

With this she drew away from me and went back to her sobbing and wailing and slapping of the cheeks.

It Can Only Be a Dream

We arrived early and were told to wait outside in the yard. I was accompanying a neighbour whose fifteen-year-old daughter was being tried by the Ramallah military court for throwing stones at a Jewish settler's pick-up van. I had volunteered to come with her to translate the court proceedings and to support her through the ordeal.

We waited for the military judges outside the Tegart* build-

---

*Charles Tegart was a British mandatory engineer who designed police stations that were built all over Palestine in 1938–9. The buildings in the West Bank now house the headquarters of the Israeli military government.

ing – perched on the Ramallah hill near the radio station and surrounded by houses sprouting television antennae shaped like Eiffel Towers. The yard is closed off with barbed wire, and many women were sitting cross-legged on the ground, waiting to attend the trials of their sons and daughters or to visit them in jail. I noticed that this Tegart – like the other little Bastilles set up all over the West Bank – has undergone a face-lift. Everything looked spick and span, fresh whitewash, tidy yard.

It was a beautiful winter's day, cold but crisp, with brilliant clear sunshine. You could see the hills for miles around, folding and unfolding in changing pastel shades of pink and grey.

After some time we were ushered into the empty courtroom and told to extinguish our cigarettes. Thirteen other girls were also on trial and we squashed on to the bench with the mothers and other relatives, waiting in hushed silence.

The young soldier shouted and we heard the judge thump in in heavy army boots. 'All stand!' the soldier roared. We stood until the judge had seated himself, and the trial began.

It was then that I had the vivid, strange certainty that I was dreaming, that this was not real. This feeling always hovers in the background – no matter how deeply we are affected by these strangers on our land – but now the feeling took complete possession.

I looked at the judge: a young Polish-born officer, his tight uniform exposing the lines of his healthy body, stared unabashedly, blankly at us, his audience – an exuberant, cheerful soldier perched on the judge's pedestal in front of the symbol of *Zva Hahagana Leyisrael* (Israel Defence Forces).

The gum-chewing prosecutor, a young Israeli lawyer doing his army service, calls a witness to the stand. Shoshana of Ofra* has long black braids and answers the prosecutor's questions in a sleepy, Russian-accented drawl. She looks

---

*Ofra is one of the first Jewish settlement established on the West Bank, known for its violence towards villagers in its vicinity.

17

lazily at the prosecutor's pencil pointing at her and says: 'I have been living in Ofra for a year. I was driving to work in my Fiat when some schoolgirls threw stones at me.'

She tosses her braids over her shoulders for a brief glance at the girls in their school uniforms bunched up together in the dock and, pointing at them, she faces the prosecutor again and says: 'It was those girls.'

The girls fidget in their seats. 'God help us!' cry their mothers, sitting on the bench beside me.

The dashingly dressed Israeli Communist defence attorney, who often takes up cases on behalf of samidīn, gets up to cross-examine, heavy make-up glittering, bracelets dangling. She speaks in a loud voice, but it doesn't help the mothers; they don't understand Hebrew.

She fires questions at Shoshana: 'You drive every day on the road from Ofra to Beit El? You have seen these girls before? You work in the military government? You have a radio and listen to the news? Did you hear there was a strike to protest against Ofra settlers smashing villagers' sheds? Do you know you are illegally occupying the land that rightly belongs to these girls?'

The law-student prosecutor takes the pencil out of his mouth, hitches up his trousers and makes an objection. And all three, the prosecutor, the judge, the defence lawyer, draw close together. They speak in a foreign tongue, a secret language, and come to a conclusion. The girls do not stir. The audience holds its breath and no one knows what has happened.

Then more questions are asked and answered. The soldier standing guard near the accused girls is bored and he stands up and turns to leave. It is cold in this courtroom. He wants to go out and stand under the sun in the prisoners' yard. Just before he leaves he remembers to salute his superior in rank, the judge. The door slams shut behind him.

The girls giggle, pull themselves together and assume a more serious demeanour. The Red Cross delegate puts his ear close to the mouth of his elegant interpreter whose hands are buried in her beige sweater and whose head is tucked into its long turtleneck against the cold. The delegate doesn't want to miss a word and the judge is careful not to commit any procedural blunders.

The defence lawyer goes on cross-examining the witness. Shoshana of Ofra answers the questions laconically.

I sit with the mothers who are more baffled than ever by this ordeal their daughters are putting them through. My translations don't help. Then the judge raises his voice: the case is adjourned.

We troop out into the sunlit yard, a relief after the cold courtroom. We stand there for a while; I try to explain a bit of what is happening, warn them about the verdict that is likely. But my mind is on Shoshana. Here, near Ramallah, a Russian lives in a settlement, uses our soil at the back of her prefabricated cottage to plant tomatoes, onions and mint, raises children, travels every day through our towns and villages to and from work in the military government; and now she stands in this Bastille and, with one lazy sweep of her hand, seals the fate of these girls in a trial staged by her people – the strangers. When did this dream begin?

Postscript

The verdict was not given until several days later. As expected, the girls were found guilty and were sentenced to five months in prison and were fined the enormous sum of 5,000 Israeli pounds, which their parents would have to provide.

The Green Kufiyeh

Looking at the twinkling lights of the Mediterranean coast on the horizon last night, I remembered how I felt many years ago as I was preparing to go for my day off – away from the land of my sumūd, into the land of the old-time samidīn: to il-Lid,* Ramleh, Yāfā,† Haifa and 'Akka‡ (their very names are music to me).

Whenever there was an electric-power failure in Ramallah, I would look with envy and admiration at the land to the west that my parents had left, the magical dream-world of my childhood. It wasn't the first time that I would be going across, but the defeat was still too close for me to feel its full impact, and I was very excited.

In the morning, I checked the most important item of all, my identity card – without it I could end up in jail – and set off. I remember vividly the joy I felt, doing the prohibited, as I drove deeper and deeper through the hills towards Latrun – the 1948–67 armistice line. It is a beautiful road, meandering through the high hills, passing through Upper Beit-'Ur and then descending to the lower village of the same name. The terraced terrain, covered in olive trees, looks as if it was squeezed by a giant hand and was then left to unfurl at its leisure. The land beyond Lower Beit-'Ur has escaped the scoop of the mighty hand. The fields stretch more gracefully, only slightly curled, covered by a deep green, almost velvety, soft grass, with only a few stones protruding.

I stopped my car near the Latrun Monastery, on the old armistice line, the border that once divided me from the coast. The rocky brown fields of the foetus-shaped West Bank, resting uncomfortably in Israel's belly, lay behind me. A sweet breeze swept my face as I prepared to make the crossing into this other world of blessed, fertile fields.

*Lydda.   †Jaffa.   ‡Acre.

I remember how, driving along the road to Jaffa, intoxicated by the smell of the orange orchards, my heart suddenly began beating what was by then the familiar tune of life on the West Bank – I saw the checkpoint ahead of me.

'*Boker Tov* [Good morning],' I said in my best Hebrew.

'*Boker Ohr* [Good morning],' the guard answered, and looked closely at my face.

'*Shalom* [Goodbye],' he said, waving me through with his hand.

It is uncomfortable now to remember the gloating feeling of satisfaction I experienced at having slid by, thinking: 'That's good! He must have taken me for a Jew because of my East Jerusalem licence plate.' I felt the shame then, only seconds after my little victory, and then the kick of revolt – I can't stand up and assert my Palestinian identity every day – damn pride and politics – I'm doing what none of those who fled to Jordan can do, however much they scorn us and laugh at us. They can't come here as I do and see our parents' land.

For all that bravado, my enchantment must have faded by the time I reached Jaffa. I had intended a grand tour, beginning with my parents' home which they fled in 1948, of the landmarks in my favourite childhood stories. But, directly after parking the car, I ran into a tourist group and heard the guide's explanations. And I saw through his listeners' eyes the 'cute' Israeli 'reconstructions' of Old Jaffa: the site of my romantic longings, plastered over into art galleries, discos, expensive restaurants, fancy shops. No tourist or Israeli my age could ever guess that thirty-five years ago this was the vibrant, flourishing Arab centre of Palestine. No trace of it is left; its people are scattered all over the world.

More than anything, I recall the feeling of deep, very deep humiliation as I quickly got back into the car and drove away. I decided to continue my tour, to Acre, but its colour had changed.

I stopped off in Tel Aviv for lunch – to see the Israelis in their natural habitat. The faces, the walk of the women and the men seemed so confident, loud – the self-contained assuredness of a victorious people. The young state takes good care of its young people, in return for their serving the flag. These healthy, vibrant faces contrasted sharply in my mind with the withdrawn, beaten faces I had left behind me on the West Bank.

As I parked, an old man wrote down my licence-plate number. I wondered whether he was off to call the police or was storing the information against the time when a bomb would go off. In the bar, there was an Argentinian woman, and the waiter also seemed to be from Latin America. They were talking animatedly in Spanish, with some Hebrew words interspersed. She spoke with her fingers, like an Arab. They seemed to be discovering that they shared many experiences – after being brought here from thousands of miles away to start a new life. They were talking about washing-machines, I think, tax-free benefits they got as new immigrants.

I left Tel Aviv and travelled through Haifa to Acre, to visit the houses where some relatives of mine had lived. Again I saw a ghost of a dream. An ancient, heroic, now humiliated city. The walls were full of graffiti: '*Allahu – Akbar!* [God is almighty!]' On sale in one of the tourist shops in the old city I saw a green kufiyeh – the black-and-white symbol of Palestinian resistance dyed a pretty green to sell to tourists.

There were more Arabs here than I had seen in Jaffa or Haifa. But they had nothing to say to me. They turned their backs on me, busy mending their fishing nets. These fishermen had carried on fishing, struggling alone, abandoned by other Arabs, since 1948. I think this was the first time I fully grasped how difficult their life must have been. I knew too that they would find it hard to believe that I understood. We have been as insensitive to them as some of our brothers in Jordan are now towards us.

I passed them silently and stood facing the breakers on the west. The waves were breaking angrily at the foot of the sea wall, and the spray reached my face. All my life I had had the dream of living on this coast – the land of my father. Now I was on it, my face was wet with spray, and it was more inaccessible than ever.

Ramallah was engulfed in fog when I returned. It was already dark. Everyone was in his house: no one could be seen and no one heard. I felt that I had left another world. Yet this world I returned to buzzed with a familiar sound. Without hearing them speak, I knew what my people wanted to say. Without seeing them act, I knew what they wanted to do. Together we were one in our sumūd. The life we shared under occupation made us a people that no physical force or clever tactic could destroy.

I drove through the foggy, deserted streets and in the distance I saw a blinking light. I stopped, and an Arab policeman asked me for my identity card. There was no question about my identity. . . I was back home.

Khalil

Khalil is out of jail. I went to his village, 'Isawiyyeh, to welcome him home.

I had never been to 'Isawiyyeh before. I drove to the concrete jungle Israel has built on Mount Scopus in East Jerusalem – the new Hebrew University buildings and the densely built residential towers of the French Hill. I knew 'Isawiyyeh was hidden somewhere below, and I stopped someone and asked him how to get there. He gave me detailed instructions, but still I lost my way. Every time I thought I was on the road out, it somehow turned back on itself, leading deeper and deeper into the maze. I was closed in by columns of windowless towering monsters, covered in glaring white, machine-sawed stone facing.

I don't know how, but suddenly I found I was on a road leading out towards a village, into another world, with terraced houses merging softly with the round hills they hugged . . . a scattering of tiny, man-made homes, tucked away below the Israeli fortresses.

In the village, everyone knew where Khalil lived. I climbed up to his house and found it full of well-wishers, plying him with questions and celebrating his return to freedom.

Khalil was sixteen the last time I saw him. He was imprisoned under a clause in the Emergency Regulations dating from the British Mandate, concerning membership in an illegal organization. His face was smooth then, but five years later I see that my young friend could easily be taken for thirty.

I had been expecting an emotional reunion. I found Khalil subdued and myself lost for the right words with which to begin. There were many people present and he had to entertain them. This gave me time to watch him. He seemed nervous with his guests. I thought of what he had missed, how during these years I have slowly grown into the adult society here, acquiring a social and professional face to use among my fellow samidīn and towards our occupiers. Khalil has none of this. He seems raw – his movements are abrupt, angry, and he looks lost.

Only after most of the people had left did we have a chance to be alone together. We went into his room and he showed me pictures of his friends in jail. He began to speak haltingly. 'I entered prison a boy. People now regard me as a man, being in prison qualifies me for that. I am expected to behave as a grown man, yet I feel so strange, as if my life has missed many turns.'

'What do you plan to do with yourself now?' I asked Khalil.

'All the time I was in jail, I was dreaming of ploughing and planting my father's land. That was all I could think of – the sun, the air, feeling the soil.' Khalil's voice trailed off.

Suddenly I remembered that his father's land had been expropriated by the Israelis. It was now hidden under buildings like those I had just escaped from on Mount Scopus. I was sorry for my thoughtlessness and said quickly: 'I didn't mean to press you. I imagine that for the time being you have no plans, that you just want to enjoy your freedom.'

Khalil did not answer. He began talking about life in prison, about the friends he had made, the men he admired. It was clear that the veteran political prisoners amongst them had left their mark on him, moulding his perceptions of us outside. He gave me to understand that he did not think much of us, nor of the freedom that he was being welcomed back into.

At one stage he said: 'What is this freedom that you think you have? Can you travel abroad without getting a permit from the army? Would you be granted one if you were out of favour with the authorities? Can you buy land, register a company or even get a telephone without the permission of some military officer or other? And everyone is frightened. Scared that if they make the wrong move they will land in jail. Well, I can tell you. At least in prison you are not afraid. You have nothing to lose. It is there that you find the brave men. And it is they who are really free.'

I had heard talk in this vein from Palestinian jail veterans who had been in and out of prison since the occupation and before. I had also heard the accusations that Khalil produced as the night wore on: that we samidīn had become scared of our own shadows; that we had lost our pride, that it was we who really punish those amongst us who are brave enough to follow their conscience and risk jail. We shed a tear over our heroes, rely on them to keep up the myth of the Palestinian resistance, but turn a cold shoulder on them as soon as they are caught, as soon as it becomes dangerous.

There is usually a bitter, distorted arrogance in such accusations that makes me discount them. But something in Khalil's youthfulness, his obvious pain and confusion, left me exposed, gave a sharp twist to doubts that are never far from the surface.

But mostly it is of Khalil that I have been thinking. A friend told me on the drive back that, ever since his release, he gets up early with the cries of the mu'azin,* makes his bed meticulously, and then sits down on it and begins poring over photographs of his friends in prison. He hates to go outside. When Khalil went to prison, the Hebrew University had not yet been built; now it chokes his village, and the sight of those buildings drives him into rages and he shuts himself up in his room. And with everything he does, it is clear that part of him is still with his friends in prison, where life was in many ways so much simpler.

And in other, more objective ways, Khalil's prison term has not yet ended. As with other released West Bank prisoners, his identity card was stamped on each corner with a triangle enclosed in a circle. When he presents his card at checkpoints or when he uses it to apply for a job, a place in the university, a licence, a travel permit, etc., he will be singled out and most of his requests turned down. And if he applies for a new card, it too will be stamped on four corners.

It is true that everyone here on the West Bank is severely restricted: but there are degrees, and Khalil has much more suffering in store for him than most of us.

There is an option open to Khalil. He can go to the Allenby Bridge on the Jordan River, hand in his identity card and sign a paper which says that he forfeits the right to return to this land of sumūd. Many break in this way. But this is a road to freedom that Khalil would never choose.

---

*The mosque crier who calls for prayers five times a day. Often spelt in English 'muezzin'.

Colonized

Today I visited an old friend of the family who works in the Department of Agriculture. His father used to own hundreds of dunums near Beer es-Sabā (Beersheba), but when they moved to Jericho in 1948, the land was taken over by the Custodian of Absentee Property and was never regained. The old man did not buy any more land, to the distress of our friend who had studied agriculture and has nowhere to apply his knowledge. Instead, he works in the department.

I was shocked by the state of his office. I had visited him there several years before, when the Israelis were still proud to have local Arabs working under their supervision. They not only kept up the standard of the Jordanian institutions – they even sought to improve them. The policy then was to encourage Israeli-Arab cooperation. The Arab employees were sent on courses in Israel and were invited to take part in conferences on modern agricultural techniques.

But now, technical cooperation is discouraged here, as everywhere. The budget has been slashed severely and many employees from Jordanian times have been fired. And this was to be expected. For it is clearly against the interests of a government that wants to take over the land to encourage local residents to become better farmers: this would only strengthen their ties to the land. More efficient farming would also deprive Israel of the cheap labour that it needs by now. The many labourers who are bussed over to Israel from the occupied territories every morning are not encouraged to earn their living from their own land.

Deterioration and poverty were much in evidence when I walked into my friend's office. It was shabby and unkempt, with mounds of dusty papers covering the desks. I found him looking harried, with at least a dozen men clustering around him like beggars.

He asked me to wait in the other room, and joined me ten

minutes later. He was immediately followed by four men.

He gave me an apologetic smile. 'May I bring you some coffee, or perhaps tea?' he asked.

'No thank you, Hatim, I have just drunk some coffee,' I said.

'Listen, I have told you a hundred times,' my friend went on, turning distractedly to one of the men who had followed him. 'I cannot give your cousin *mu'an* [rations] because she has not registered with us.'

'But she has registered,' the man lied, looking my friend blankly in the eye.

'Let's not play games. Where is her name on the list? Is she called Sabha, Fatmeh, 'Aisheh, eh?' My friend read on down the list. Suddenly he stopped, sorry for his loss of patience, and said gently to the man, what he must have said scores of times before: 'Only someone who owns cattle and has registered with the department that he has inoculated his cattle is eligible for *mu'an*. Your cousin has not registered and she does not have cattle. She cannot be given a ration.'

The old man, dressed in a tattered *jallabiyyeh*, smiled at my friend's explanation, which he seemed to let him finish only out of politeness, and repeated, as if nothing had been said: 'But she has registered.' He waved a painfully bad forgery of a card in my friend's face.

My friend looked exhausted, but he was not angry. Although only in his late thirties, he had an almost grandfatherly air. His light, benevolent eyes were buried in swollen cheeks. For a moment he looked like a missionary, come to work among the natives. But, of course, he is no missionary. It is lucky we still have a few of our well-intentioned people working in such thankless tasks, having to represent to their own people a military government that has deprived their jobs of any substance.

The *mukhtar* was amongst the petitioners, several more of whom had invaded the room. He addressed my friend by his title and raised his hand, like a schoolboy asking for permission to speak. He pulled faces to hide the lies he was telling. They all looked undernourished and miserable, completely absorbed in the fight for survival, which at this moment meant lying, wheedling and currying favour with Hatim. Hatim made promises that I knew he could not keep, and they were comforted and flattered but they showed no indication of leaving.

My friend grew uneasy on my behalf. He pointed at me and said: 'This is the man who brings all the rations. He is the doctor, all the rations come from him.'

They looked at my glasses and believed him. They turned on me, and I was surrounded by beseeching faces, hands tugging at my clothes for attention. I assumed a stern, pompous tone and ordered them out, after explaining that there were no rations today and that their conduct would be detrimental to receiving them later. They accepted my authority and slunk away.

My friend and I did not enjoy our easily gained respite. How painfully and degradingly simple it is to outwit our people. And how easy it must be for the Israelis. No effort is needed to control a society so geared to paternalism that it barely matters who the authority is which does the ordering. We manipulate and defer to authority so naturally that we do not even see the humiliation and the shame. The Israelis need only slide into the waiting slot to reap all the benefits.

And they do. Advising the military governors are 'experts on Arab mentality' churned out by the Hebrew University and called 'advisers on Arab affairs'. These experts have at their fingertips all there is to be known about our dialects, habits, affiliations, feuds and hierarchies. Their job is to utilize this vast knowledge to create and sustain divisions to make their rule easier – ensuring that each one of us has a role to play in their scheme. Today, I fitted in beautifully.

Sāmid for How Long?

The Israeli occupation of the West Bank makes international headlines when houses are demolished, samidīn expelled and demonstrations dispersed with violence. But it is more often the accumulation of the daily petty humiliations that makes a Sāmid or Sāmdeh crack under the strain.

Road-blocks: West Bankers and residents of the Gaza Strip have blue and white licence-plates respectively, to single them out from the yellow-plated cars of their Israeli counterparts. On the blue and white plates, on the left-hand-side corner, is a Hebrew letter, the first letter of the Hebrew name of the driver's town. Each town's special letter is in a different colour. The licence-plates make the job of singling out an Arab driver easy. They are usually automatically stopped and searched at road-blocks, while the Israeli drivers are waved through. The East Jerusalem plates are yellow, like the Israelis'; they are distinguishable only by their first two numbers. This is not so eye-catching, and sometimes a busy or tired guard mistakes you for an Israeli and waves you through.

Some road-blocks are permanent, in Israel, but mainly in the occupied territories; others are put up for specific purposes. I often think that, unlike many fedayeen who join the armed struggle for noble and weighty reasons, if I ever find myself on the other bank of the Jordan River it will be because my luck in getting through road-blocks with my sanity intact has run out.

Yesterday, my mother and I scraped through one precariously – thanks to my mechanical ineptitude. Looking back on it, it takes on a farcical, mad coloration, like all dangerous confrontations that are bumblingly survived.

I was driving my mother to the Lydda Airport near Tel Aviv to meet my brother who was due to arrive in the evening from the USA, where he had been studying for over a year. At the airport we were stopped by a soldier, given the routine check for Arabs, and then allowed through. The plane was delayed by several hours, so we decided to go to Tel Aviv for supper. On the way back to the airport I lost my way, as I invariably do when trying to negotiate the highway between Tel Aviv and the airport.

So it was quite late when we drove in to the checkpoint. There was something strange about the soldier manning it. He had very pale blue eyes and a puffy red face. He told us to draw up on the roadside and ordered us to get out of the car. His movements were crude and his tone more stupidly insulting than is usual. After checking our identity papers and conducting a very thorough body-search, he began a methodical examination of the contents of the car. Unfortunately, the car was full of bags of shopping and other things, and I could see that the soldier was settling in for a long session. I told him we would be late for my brother's plane, which seemed only to slow him down further.

We finally reached the boot of the car. 'What's this?' he asked, pointing at a huge sack of soil that I had bought the day before for my garden in Jericho and had been too lazy to take out of the car.

'Soil,' I said.

'Pour it out!' he barked.

'Where?' I asked. I suspected he wanted me to dump it out on to the floor of the boot and I was damned if I was going to.

I must have struck him as insolent because he exploded with curses. I can't say why now, but I persisted; finally, perhaps out of surprise at my insistence, he accepted a compromise solution: I would pour it out, but on the tarmac rather than in the boot. This done, he wanted to move on to something else, apparently intending to leave the soil on the road for posterity. I was loath to lose the good soil and said I wanted to put it back in the sack. It must have dawned on him that this would delay us still further, because he quickly agreed to my request but insisted that my mother help me, prodding me with his gun when I objected.

My mother and I scooped up what we could salvage. We

straightened our backs and there was a moment's eerie silence as the three of us stood grouped under the neon light, late at night, with not a soul in sight. The soldier's pale, neurotic eyes, sweating face and dangling gun gleamed in the strange purple light. The common procedures of road-blocks and the game we were all supposed to play (it is for our own good, needless to say, that we are stopped) no longer applied. The veneer of common sense that somehow coats this violent apprehension of one human by another had long since cracked. This soldier was indulging his private sadism with legally supplied victims and making no secret of his intention to satisfy his urges.

I could sense my mother's growing fear. With a last gesture towards the idea that the law is there to protect us all, I flagged down a passing police car. I began to explain, rationally, I thought, that the soldier was exceeding the accepted road-block procedures. The policeman did not let me finish my sentence. He seemed outraged that an Arab should dare query the conduct of a Jewish soldier. He screamed at me to get back to the car, winked at the soldier and drove away.

It was fury and shame at my helplessness in protecting my mother rather than fear that I now had to keep under control. I heard the soldier sniggering and ordering me to unscrew the spare wheel.

Now, I am no mechanic and I really did not know how to go about it. The soldier was furious and incredulous by turns – apparently he could not believe that anyone could be so stupid. He was spluttering and looking dangerous, so to calm him down I suggested that I follow the instructions in the manual. I opened it to the page entitled 'Wheel Changing' and began to read. Every instruction had bracketed references to numbers which were matched with pictures on the opposite page. 'Take out the wheel jack (1) and (2). Unscrew the spare wheel carrier nut (3) (about 15 turns) with the brace. Lift the hatch (4) to free the carrier. . .' I went on, step by step – the diagrams were a great help. The soldier, I noticed, had stopped pacing up and down and cursing. Perhaps he was bored, waiting for me to unravel the instructions, because I felt him leaning over me, apparently absorbed, correcting me where I went wrong.

The wheel finally came off. It had barely touched the ground when he said: 'Now put it back on.'

Again I referred to the manual. This seemed a much more complicated task. I fiddled about aimlessly until the soldier grabbed the booklet from my hand and tried to make sense of the instructions himself. This went on for quite a while. The danger had disappeared for the moment – the soldier seemed as exhausted and exasperated as I was, and was probably regretting he had ever embarked on the search. At any rate, he raised no objection when I suggested we flag down a taxi and ask for help.

A driver stopped and began helping us with the wheel. He seemed apologetic and said a curt word to the soldier about making a mother and son go through this rigmarole.

Some more cars stopped, and as my mother began recounting the ordeal, they all appeared embarrassed. One of them tried to explain to me that my soldier was 'overworked'.

A police car stopped, probably because of the crowd. My mother went up to him to complain. He, too, seemed uneasy. He said: 'Madame, you must realize that there are many hashish smugglers and we can't be too careful.' Of course. He took our identity papers away from the soldier and handed them back to us. But the taxi-driver had already broken the soldier's hold on us.

My mother would have stayed on to complain; but I was not interested in explanations about the soldier's workload. They only increased my fury at the law singling us out as offerings for such creatures to do with us as they like. I drove away quickly – fleeing while I still had my feathers.

Enoch

I met Enoch several years ago in Tel Aviv, at a New Outlook conference. There were many Palestinians and many Israelis and many speeches. The conference coincided with Anwar Sadat's visit to Jerusalem, and the high point was his televised speech to the Knesset. This was naturally followed by heated discussions, which later continued among small groups of people. Enoch and I found ourselves in one of these discussion groups and somehow stayed alone in a room and talked. Of everything but politics.

We met as two individuals in the middle of a political 'get together' – and that is how we have remained through the years: great friends in a world where Palestinians and Israelis can meet only as political representatives of their respective peoples.

It sounds so normal: two people meet, like each other, become friends. But this natural process rarely occurs in our abnormal world because the walls of mistrust that enclose us are so impenetrable that it is almost impossible to fight your way through them. Enoch's warmth, honesty and humour just dissolved those walls from the very beginning, dissolved the stifling caution that we samidīn use to protect ourselves in our relations with Israelis.

Like other samidīn, I have acquired – in addition to the straightforward mistrust of the colonizer's smile – a deeper and more painful suspicion of friendly overtures made by Israelis who proclaim themselves against the occupation. For it very often happens that the gesture of friendship is no more than a request for a pat on the back to salve the unhappy Israeli's conscience, or else you are being used as fodder for someone with a theory of world revolution, etc. To protect myself from this, I have learnt through the years to restrict conversation in all such encounters to immediate politics and policies – relatively safe common ground: safe in the sense that things can be spelt out clearly; safe in that this leaves out all personal feelings and far-reaching ideologies. If you let go of this, all the distortions of guilt, fear and resentment begin to surface, and even this minimal communication becomes impossible.

With Enoch, things were quite different. We began as personal friends and slowly, as our trust in each other grew, we faced up to, and confronted, each other with the feelings that we each have as members of our warring peoples. This has often been difficult, but so far has only deepened our friendship. Much of our time together we spend on long, rambling walks. I readily accepted Enoch's own peculiar, often wild love of the land. For his is not the jealous, possessive kind you find in most Israelis. Enoch, for all that he is a serious biblical scholar and loves the land of the Jewish Bible, loves also the land of the New Testament and the land of the Arabs. And so we roam the hills and the coast on a private trail of our own making – a mixture of his and my dreams, imaginings and histories.

It is not only Enoch's gentleness and far-flung imagination and knowledge that come out in the way he loves our land. It is also his freedom from fears that stamp both Arabs and Jews. A few days ago, he turned up at my place with a sleeping bag. He was off, he said, to sleep 'somewhere near the Latrun Monastery'. I began clucking like an anxious hen – nobody would dare do that. But he just laughed his gentle laugh, amused, and off he went. I should be used to him by now. One evening, quite early on in our friendship, after visiting the Church of the Nativity in Bethlehem together, he announced that he was going on to Hebron. At first I thought that he had friends in the Jewish settlement of Kiryat Arba, just outside Hebron. But to my relief he said: no, he was going to take a bus and find a place to stay overnight in Hebron. There are no hostels or hotels in Hebron, I explained, and it is not safe for a Jew or an Arab to go there at night. But he would not listen; when I spoke to him next, he said that when he got there he had made friends with an Arab family and stayed with them at their house for several days.

It was only after our first meeting that I learned that Enoch, who is a psychiatrist by profession, and I were both 'green'. I had just returned to the West Bank after several years of study in England, and he had quite recently come to Israel from Canada. His mother, whom he adored, was a fervent Zionist. When she died he came to Israel to carry out her dream. He did not like what he saw – he regarded much of modern Israel as a betrayal of what he valued in Judaism. But he did not feel free to walk away, because he saw the relations between Jews and Arabs as the moral test that Judaism must pass. I think that this is our deepest bond – our determination, on either side of the fence, to persist, not to pack up our bags and leave the land we love in the hands of those who are driving us to war.

Enoch does not expect me to forget, when we laugh and walk together, nor does he forget himself, the accumulation through the years of the wrongs that his people have done to mine . . . no more than I expect him to forget the terrible sufferings of his people. And here, too, Enoch's attitude is rare. Most well-meaning Israelis adopt a stance of 'forgive and forget' on meeting samidīn – but without any knowledge of what they are asking us to forget. They mean that we should forgive and forget things that they don't even bother to know about, things that happened to us because they came here.

It was because Enoch forgets neither his nor my people's suffering – without entering into an obscene competition of who suffered more – that I have learned from him to be open to, and feel deeply, the past history of the Jews and what Israel means to them. It is due to him that I have come to accept that the Palestinians will have to sacrifice a lot for peace: we will have to learn to share our land with the Jews in pre-'67 Israel – those who have settled in the Jaffa that my parents left and on land where whole villages of ours have been wiped out.

But there is something sadly paradoxical in my learning this from Enoch, because the deep trust I have in him, which made me see this, is an exception to the rule. And often there is a feeling about our friendship of time borrowed until we are each thrust into the role of being soldiers in the bloody war that will rage for a long time between our peoples.

Enoch once wrote to me: 'When I think of Enoch the individual meeting Raja the individual I feel no tension. When I think of Enoch the Jew encountering Raja the Palestinian, I feel the tension of conflict of interest, of history, of murder. At first, I feel anger because the political situation may rob me of Raja my friend, because I can no longer meet him under these conditions, and because under these conditions my friend will cease to exist. But in more optimistic moods, I believe that I will be able to meet Raja the Palestinian as a friend and as a comrade. Yet, we are not masters of our own fate.'

And it is this oscillation between hope and despair that hovers over the times we spend together.

It is hard by now to think that a political solution is going to work here – certainly not before much blood is spilt. Enoch speaks of the 'demonic, subterranean' vengeance and fear that drive both of our peoples. And he wrote: 'After so much suffering, killing, distrust – there need to be some rituals of truce, of mutual confessions of wrongdoing, so that a more genuine intimacy may grow on the seedbed of despair. In short, we must beg each other's forgiveness, and if people cannot come in their pride to humble themselves before one another, then perhaps we can all, in our own way but together, ask forgiveness from a higher power.'

Enoch is religious in an unusual way and he believes in this higher power. But I must make do with my belief in man; perhaps for that reason my despair is sometimes greater than his.

I have been with Enoch to Yad Vashem, the memorial for the six million Jews exterminated by the Nazis. It was there that

Enoch taught me the wisdom of the inmates of the Treblinka concentration camp: 'Faced with two alternatives, always choose the third.'

Like many Palestinians, I used to see it as inevitable that the survivors of the holocaust would be driven by such hate and fear that they would act ruthlessly to ensure their own preservation, regardless of who paid for it. But Enoch remembers the evil perpetrated against his people, remembers it deeply, without himself being a hate-blinded, vengeance-seeking victim of that wrong. In him I see that really honouring the memory of people who have suffered creates courage and a capacity for love that cannot be equalled by someone who does not remember or acknowledge man's capacity for evil. What I have learned from Enoch has made me expect more from the Jews – which is not easy because it opens a place for hope and its betrayal. But even more importantly, it has taught me to expect more of myself: never to excuse in myself the psychology of a victim – someone whose actions and reactions you can understand, in the circumstances, but not respect.

Enoch speaks much of the 'third way'. I am not sure I understand fully what it means to him, but I think that it is close to much that I myself seek as Sāmid. For Enoch, I know that the third way is God's way – one which he must discover and follow in order to avoid being trapped into accepting the choice between two wrong alternatives. But I cannot think of it as God's path that is out there, beckoning, waiting to be discovered. It must, for me, be something that is created as I go along, forged step by step while I live here as Sāmid.

I think a lot about the choice that samidīn feel cornered into making: exile or submissive capitulation to the occupation, on the one hand – or blind, consuming hate and avenging the wrongs done to them, on the other. But it is in this conception of choice that the trap lies. States of mind cannot be forced on you. This is where you are free, your own master – because your mind is the one thing that you can prevent your oppressor from having the power to touch, however strong and brutal he may be. If he has touched it, that is when you have been defeated, and that is when you become a predictable puppet, a bundle of psychological characteristics which the experts can study and use for their own purposes. I know that my Israeli occupiers want me in this state – want me to believe that vengeance and submission are my only alternatives. I know too that I am close to defeat when I feel driven by them, scarcely recognizing that these are *their* alternatives, not *mine*.

All of this is difficult to express and even more difficult, almost impossible to live by. But I must succeed in order to be Sāmid. For it is this freedom that is most vulnerable under the long-drawn-out occupation, with no end in sight but war. And even that end, which I dread, may take a long time in coming. It is the day-to-day living that is the test of sumūd. And I know that I fail very often.

Spring 1980 Journal

April 24
I saw Subhi this morning in the street and he told me about last night, in a halting voice, as if he was trying to describe a nightmare that he could not quite believe.

> It was hot and I couldn't get to sleep. I opened the windows for some breeze. Then the mating cats kept me awake. Next thing I know, I hear this screeching sound. I thought it must be the cats. I woke up – it was glass, breaking glass. I got up to see what it was, looked out of the balcony. Saw this truck, van, coming slowly down the street. There were hands stretched out of the back – each grasping a stone. All the hands moved together – another crash – they broke the windows of Samān's car. They were coming down the street – smashing every parked car. It was dark except for their headlights. Then they got Khalid's car, then George's. I could see my beautiful Fiat was next. Nobody dares touch it. Then I saw its window smashing – stones, more stones. I screamed. I heard some voices shouting in Hebrew – a stone flew through the balcony. I ducked in time – it crashed into the lamp in our living room. I wanted to wake my brother. But what could we do? Those men in the van must be armed. I could hear them shouting. Would they climb upstairs and rape 'Aisheh? I checked that the doors were locked. I took a kitchen knife and waited for them. They didn't come. The papers say they were Gush Emunim people – they want to take the law in their own hands. They say this is just the beginning.

Subhi walked off. I saw him go up to someone else and tell his story again. I continued down the street: 150 cars were smashed last night in Ramallah and El-Bireh by Gush Emunim people on a vengeance spree. Fear of the paramilitary – who we shall now have to deal with as well as the army – is in everyone's talk, on all faces.

April 28
Meir Kahane of the Jewish ultra-nationalist Kach movement came to Ramallah today with some of his followers. He marched up to the town hall to deliver the following message: 'The Arabs of Eretz Israel [Palestine] constitute a time-bomb for the Jewish state. The only solution is for the Arabs to be sent out of here to the Arab states and to the West, and for the Jews of the world to be brought to Israel – this is the only way.' Then they handed out leaflets – in Hebrew – repeating this message to the people of our town.

In 1948 a young Jewish girl stood in the middle of Deir Yassin and warned the villagers that unless they left they would be massacred. Next day, the Irgun terrorists slaughtered 250 residents of the village. The man who was then head of the Irgun is now the head of Israel's government. Is that what Kahane's visit meant? I cannot, must not, believe that. But if I don't flee, if I remain Sāmid, will they say of me tomorrow that I went like a lamb to the slaughter?

A crowd gathered near the town hall to protest against Kahane's visit. This afternoon, I learnt that Hani [the writer's fifteen-year-old neighbour] was shot in the leg by a soldier. There are many stories circulating about how it happened. Apparently he got caught up in this morning's demonstration. The soldiers dispersed the demonstration and fired down the alleys at the crowd. Munir [a doctor in the Ramallah Hospital] told me that the army would not let Hani be treated in Ramallah, and that he was taken in an ambulance to Jerusalem. His mother went with him.

April 29
Every day now, you see or read and hear about clashes between the Israeli settlers and soldiers, and West Bank schoolchildren and students. The Jews have stones and guns, and the Arabs have stones and they burn tyres. The roads all over the West Bank are closed. Today, soldiers stopped me on the road. Further down the road, other soldiers were herding together a group of demonstrating students. They put them on a bus and shaved each one down the middle of his head. Branded. The Israelis may be sure that each shaved head is a new fida'i.* I have seen this before, but it is extreme. When tyres are burned, soldiers usually round up everybody in the vicinity, line them up and tell them to take their shirts off. They are then ordered to wipe the road clean of the burnt debris with their shirts. Then they are marched with their shirts tied around their waists to the military governor's compound. I wonder what would happen if they did this to the ultra-orthodox demonstrators in West Jerusalem who also seem to find tyre-burning a fitting expression of their hatred for the Israeli government.

Gush Emunim is continuing to declare it has taken the law into its own hands. Private armies will roam the streets, as well as the soldiers. They have already distributed leaflets, like those we got yesterday, to the small villages near the settlements. And they say that any Arab who dares interfere with the settlement activity will be personally punished by the settlers.

April 30
It was in this land that stoning was used as a punishment. He or she upon whom the rage of the community had fallen was condemned to death by stoning. The condemned person was dragged to the centre of the town, where all the people – the old men, the women and the children – stood watching. Stones are plentiful in this rocky land, as are the vengeful

---
*Freedom fighter. Masculine singular of fedayeen.

spirits waiting to throw them. No one hears the cries of the victims, no one sheds any tears. Stones are hurled at the condemned until his skin is torn and his blood soaks the earth, but the stones bury the sight and the shouts muffle his cries. No one has any regrets, no one has any pity, and each one lives in fear of the other. For stones are plentiful in this rocky land. Several thousands of years later, we still resort to stones. We have not changed our ways.

Khalid was in the car of an Israeli friend, driving to Nablus, on his way to visit Ahmad. Suddenly he saw an Arab car blocking their way and another blocking his rear. And he saw two Arab youths throwing stones at him. The stones were breaking the windows of the car and falling on his lap and on his head and on his shoulders, and he covered his face with his hands and cried in Arabic: 'Stop! Stop! Listen to me, listen to me!' When they heard him speaking Arabic, they stopped and then vanished. 'We could have been stoned to death. I felt their anger all over my body,' he told me.

Rafiq's parents, who live alone in the outskirts of Jerusalem, heard knocking at their door at three o'clock in the morning. 'Open up! Police!' the thieves said. But Abu-Rafiq knew they were robbers and said: 'You are no police, you have come to steal.' As soon as he spoke, stones began falling on the old couple, thrown through every window of their house which was surrounded by the band of thieves. Until daybreak the old couple hid in the corner, while their house was littered with stones.

And students throw stones to keep off the soldiers who fire at them. They are lucky to have so many stones around them, for they are their only weapons. And Gush Emunim settlers use stones. They think they will drive us away. We shall bury each other in stones. We have not left the ways of our ancestors.

This biblical land is full of stones and it is to stones we still turn for our justice and law. Hard-headed and stubborn we are, and we have not learnt any lessons.

May 1
I have just come back from visiting Hani's mother. It is late – she has been spending every day in the Hadassah Hospital in Jerusalem. It looks bad – his leg is shredded, apparently by a dum-dum bullet. The stories are still too confusing. I tried to comfort her and said all the wrong things.

Then I visited my parents' neighbour. She told me that last night the soldiers came again. It has been an almost nightly occurrence lately. When they find slogans painted on the wall, they wait until night and then wake up all the people on the street and make them whitewash the wall. Sometimes the paint isn't quite dry and, as a new layer is put on, the old layer peels away and the slogans of the previous day are revealed.

She described the scene down in the street – mainly old people wrapped in dressing-gowns, shivering, bewildered, some cursing. One woman refused to come down – the soldiers broke into her house. 'Night is the worst time. During the day you draw some comfort from the solid furniture around you. Everything looks so normal. At night you are at their mercy,' the woman said. 'But it is so easy for us, compared with the refugee camps. They don't even have the illusion of safety during the day. Nothing solid anywhere.'

It is true. The soldiers have more respect for a big town. On her street, people are well off, and I suspect that that restrains them as well. The people in the camps and the little villages are treated like animals – all night they are made to stand in the centre of the village while a house is searched. Yes, I am sure the soldiers are restrained by the money here – the refugees' homes must seem to them like the ruins they do their army practice on – just a heap of stones to be blown up.

May 3
The fedayeen attacked settlers in the centre of Hebron yesterday: six dead and sixteen wounded. Next came the Israeli response: deportation of two of our mayors and the Qadi of Hebron, and curfew imposed on Hebron. The man I stopped to buy fruit from this morning said: 'There is blood between us

and them.' By this he meant that he expects them to shoot at him now. One tribe against the other. He pointed to an Israeli civilian car and said: 'It is people like that who will shoot at us. What is to stop them? They can drive away and the army and the police won't track them down.'

He was exaggerating, of course. This is not a jungle, yet. But his is a commonly shared fear.

Hani's mother came home, exhausted, from the hospital yesterday. She was at her son's bedside when they brought in the Hebron wounded. It was like a hospital during wartime, she said. And she sat by her son's bed and was afraid. She is in the enemy's hands, she feels.

The mayors' expulsion is a significant turn in policy – part of the 'mailed fist' the Defence Ministry announced. Let terror be answered with a visibly strong hand. So many have been banished since the occupation began. But quietly, no one raised a stir, they were just taken to the border and told to walk. There is a measure of relief in it coming out into the open.

May 9
Expropriation is confirmed – 250,000 dunums of land from Burqa in the Jordan Valley. Soon all the settlers will have children born in Ofra and Ma'aleh Adunim; they will have a right of birth to stay here. Last night I dreamed that the Israelis were all over the West Bank. There were no empty virginal hills anywhere in sight. They had built many settlements: large towns, heavily industrialized, and the people covered our land, like ants. And in my dream I had no choice but to submit to their will and work in their factories. And I felt deep regret: why did we samidīn not work harder when we still had the chance to expand? Why did *we* not fill all the gaps, so that they would have no hills to settle on?

May 11
They have threatened to raze the Daheisheh refugee camp

near Bethlehem to the ground. The people of Hebron are still under curfew.

I dreamed last night that Enoch and I were trying to tell each other about a film we had both seen. I began to speak but he kept interrupting me to tell me about exactly the same film. And I interrupted him to tell him about the film. And neither of us heard the other.

May 12
On impulse, I went to see what they had done to my land. As quietly as I slid in, I slipped out. I raised no stir.

I was driving to Hebron from Bethlehem, when I suddenly decided to turn right at the sign saying ETZION MUSEUM, RESTAURANT, BUFFET. I reached the inevitable checkpoint, and prepared to be turned away. Astonishingly, I was just waved through. There were more checkpoints as I continued, and all the guards waved me on, lazily, drawing me deeper and deeper into their compound.

The houses I saw were of brick, not stone, in the style of a Florida resort motel. Neat patches of lawn, lavender bushes and children's playgrounds. There were no settlers about – only a few Arab labourers. They must only use this place in the evenings and at weekends. From where I stood I could see other settlements blooming on my hills. They will not be easy to remove. Much blood will be spilt.

On my way out, a red-eyed guard dog attacked my car. Only he felt the anger in my heart. Other than that, I raised no stir.

May 13
'Two eyes for an eye,' the Jews vowed after the Hebron massacre. The thirty days of mourning have not yet passed. When they do, we can expect blood. *The Jerusalem Post* says that the Gush Emunim settlers are preparing to fight the West Bankers, with or without the army's help, and are beginning to recruit volunteers in Israel. Regional security committees are being formed to train the newcomers.

Jonathan has been coming here every night for a month. We have had a promise that the book* will be published. The biggest difficulty is keeping it secret, explaining away exhaustion during the day. And at night, as we sit with the lights on, I feel so exposed. I have made the first moves in getting a permit to travel to Geneva, to deliver the manuscript.†

But these documents we are collecting are on the state of law, and it seems too late to speak of law now. They are just words, and it all seems too late. But we can't stop. We must not give in to the fear that silences samidīn. The world must hear what our legal system has been reduced to – hear about the violation of basic human rights. Whoever cares should know how the Israelis are cloaking their brutality in legal garb.

And for me, these nightly writing sessions have become essential. Without my writing I could not get through the days.

May 14

I was watching a group of mourners. They were sitting after the funeral on the balcony opposite mine. A warm spring breeze was blowing. Suddenly, we heard the sound of army jeeps. We saw a boy running, pursued by three soldiers. He jumped over a wall. The soldiers began talking on their walkie-talkies, and the area was surrounded. The boy was caught, and was covered in a flurry of boots and fists.

'Go inside. Inside. Go inside!' the soldiers screamed at the mourners, who were now standing, motionless, shocked. They did not see me on the opposite balcony.

Then we saw arms flashing, the boy somehow escaped the soldiers' grip. 'Shoot! Shoot!' we heard the soldiers cry. Shots followed the boy who ran in a zig-zag, like a truly expert fida'i. But the bullets caught up with him, and we saw him being

---

The West Bank and the Rule of Law, by Raja Shehadeh and Jonathan Kuttab.
†To the International Commission of Jurists.

carried by the soldiers to the jeep, with blood gushing from his head. I looked across at the mourners: one old man could not hold back his tears; they trickled down his cheeks.

May 15
I was driving with Jonathan to the land registration department in Jerusalem. The traffic was stopped while a big carrier truck carrying a whole ready-made, prefabricated house with windows, a bathroom, a living room, a kitchen, pipes – a home – was negotiating a difficult bend on the Ramallah–Jerusalem road. Then came another and a third and a fourth – six in all. We watched them drive towards one of the Jewish settlements. Near our car, a woman with her child was standing. 'See the houses of the Jews,' she said. Her son wanted to stay to watch but she snatched him away and they continued walking.

Jonathan said I should write a story: '1984 – the final evacuation of the Palestinians from the West Bank'.

We have finished everything. I am supposed to fly with the manuscript to Geneva in two days' time, but still they will not give me the *laissez-passer*. I do not know whether this is just the regular trouble they make, or whether it is because they know about the book. We are both very tense, too nervous to speak about it. And exhausted. I know they will stop me.

May 17
I am on a plane, a Swissair plane, in mid-air between Tel Aviv and Geneva. Beside me is the manuscript. I have three seats to myself. Earlier, one had been occupied by a kind, matronly woman. When I settled into the deep chair, I opened *The Jerusalem Post* and saw a report on a fida'i who got up in court and shouted 'Long live free Palestine'. He was sentenced to twenty years. And I began, ridiculously, to cry, and I couldn't stop. I don't know why. I was embarrassed. The woman next to me smiled at me and said: 'I know, I always cry when I leave Israel. It is terrible to go back to the cold world of the *goyim* [gentiles]. But it is good that we have Israel to protect us, to

make us proud. We Jews must stick together.' She offered me a piece of cake or something. For a crazy moment I longed to be taken up in her warm, ample arms. I didn't answer and must have looked strange. She soon left her seat and moved behind me. Now I hear her exchanging stories with another woman about their wonderful sabra grandchildren.

The manuscript is beside me; in two hours I will be in Geneva to hand it over for publication. I cannot believe it. I am out, free.

I haven't had any time to think what this will lead to. A report in the *Post*? Twenty years in jail? Banishment?

I can't believe we've managed to keep it a secret. How did I get out? Is one of the passengers a Mossad* man? Or maybe they are waiting for me in Geneva. It is easier abroad. But there were so many stages where they could have stopped me at home, so many stages in getting the *laissez-passer*.

First, I had to get the approval of the military governor to travel. He could have said no. Then I went to the office of the Military Officer for Civilian Affairs to submit my application. I had to go many times because the queues were very long. There were people submitting applications for family reunions, for permits for relatives to come here to visit them, for permits to travel to Jordan, for permits to go abroad . . . When I finally made it to the window and submitted my application I was told I would get the answer in a week. I went several times to check, but got no answer. Maybe they had found out. Finally, just as I was despairing, my permit was granted. And then the next stage: the most hated office in the West Bank – the population registrar. Queues much longer than those at the Department of Civilian Affairs. People, mostly from the villages around Ramallah, stand waiting, tolerating the greatest humiliation because without identity cards they can't exist. It took two weeks of going there daily, trying to make it to the door. I finally submitted my papers, plastering them with expensive revenue stamps and adding

---

*Israeli Intelligence.

my pictures. They said it would be out in two weeks.

Three weeks passed – the last three weeks. I finally decided to arrange for a meeting with the officer in charge. We reckoned that there was nothing to lose. If they knew, there was no sense in hiding. He was polite; he said I should go to the head office in Jerusalem.

The man in Jerusalem seemed friendly. I had two days to go when I saw him. In his office, there was another man who was saying how difficult it was to get a *laissez-passer* for his child – he had waited a whole week. I asked him why he needed a *laissez-passer*, he was Jewish. He said children get *laissez-passers*, not passports. Children and Arabs, I thought to myself.

Then the man who was supposed to sign my papers began to complain. He also had problems. So many applications from Arabs, so many checks to make. I was sure he meant that they had checked up on me and that he was just drawing it out, but I made sympathetic noises. He said his wife was thinking of leaving him because he cared only about his work. Five years he hadn't been on holiday, he said. I was really sorry for him by then. We talked some more and then I got so carried away that I said I was sorry to add to his burdens – I would come back tomorrow. Only when I left did I realize what had happened. It would only have taken two seconds for him to sign, yet I spent almost an hour listening to his woes. Carried away, I forgot why it was so urgent to get the *laissez-passer* immediately. I got it the following day, one day before flying.

It is brought home to me that I am not the stuff that heroes are made of. It all seems so accidental, almost despite myself, that I am here on the plane with the manuscript. Perhaps that is why I cried when I read about the fida'i in court. What on earth am I doing in his company? He knows what he is doing – determined and brave, he follows a course that he is set on – knowing the risk and willing to take it. And me – I didn't even wake up this morning for the plane. I had set two alarm clocks, but the taxi-driver who came to take me to the airport had to wake me by pounding on the door. And in the rush and confusion, I almost left the manuscript behind. But thinking back, I find this strangely reassuring. Perhaps I look too silly and distracted to be suspected.

Several days ago, towards evening, I wanted to pick some yellow flowers that I love. They have a very short flowering season and I rushed out to pick them from a place in a valley nearby. On the way, I was stopped by a soldier. There had been a demonstration earlier on in the day and soldiers were patrolling the streets, arresting people. He looked suspiciously at the scissors in my hand and said: 'Where the hell are you going with those?' I said I was going to pick some yellow flowers and he stared at me for a moment, as if I had fallen from Mars, and then shrugged his shoulders and let me go.

And maybe this is what will happen. Maybe I'll be lucky. Get away with everything without having to be a hero. I can't believe I'm in the air. In the clouds. Free. I'm not the stuff for Mossad men.

May 27
In the plane on the way back to Tel Aviv, I was dizzy with the ten days of freedom. My head was buzzing, it was like being a god. The freedom in the streets – nobody stops you, singles you out – you can go everywhere you want, no cards, numbers, road-blocks. Worked well there, finished the book, it was a pleasure, so different – no fear. Just sometimes I thought someone was following me – but it seems ridiculous there, even though I know of many who have been polished off abroad.

I was dizzy with it on the plane back. I forgot where I was heading. When I walked down the gangway, I was discreetly beckoned aside. All the passengers continued in a bus to the passenger lounge. I was taken to the side of the plane underneath the wing. I had forgotten what they do to Arabs when they land here. I have never figured out how they know who to call aside from all the passengers pouring out – I look Arab, but many don't.

And under the wings, with all the bright airplane lights glaring, I felt on a stage; I was supposed to say something but I was confused and dazed. Then I heard a voice: 'Put your hands up!', and soldiers surrounded me with guns.

I was back home. I remembered. I put up my hands and they searched me.

When they felt tubes in my pockets, they jumped back in alarm. 'Empty your pockets!' they ordered, holding on to their submachine guns.

I took out one tube of Smarties after another. I had used my last Swiss francs to buy these sweets for my brother (and myself) before leaving the airport in Geneva. The dangerous fida'i is back with his Smarties. Beware!

Then I was taken to a kind of mobile interrogation room parked near the plane. Many questions – but they didn't ask about the book. Then, I was told to get on a bus with the Swiss crew to go to the passengers' lounge. The crew were polite – had I forgotten something on the plane? Was that why I hadn't got on to the bus with the others?

'No,' I said. 'I am an Arab.'

In the passengers' lounge, I was given the pink slip for Arabs. That means a different line – the line for the interrogation room on the right-hand side of the hall. All so discreet that nobody notices. I felt for my parents out there, everybody else's son is already in their arms and they must wait for another two or three hours. I wanted to wave, but the guard said no. In the interrogation room, I found my fellow samidīn. The men in their best suits were trying to look as if it was all a joke, a mere formality, nothing to do with them personally. This is a hard face to keep up for two, three hours. The smile gets fixed. They fidget in their seats. They have been away for a long time, become used to being normal. Others already have the servile, bitter, defeated look – they have not been away from home long enough. The women with children are trying to keep them quiet. We all sit bunched up together in the room; some don't like to speak to others – they don't want to accept yet that being at home means coming back, voluntarily, to prison. The woman next to me talks. Her sister is in Hebron. The curfew has been on for almost a month. Stories of brutal house searches by soldiers. They come again and again. The people, locked in the houses, can't buy food, are not allowed out. And the soldiers pour out all the food – the rice and the flour that the people have stored up – and they mix it all up and pour olive oil over it so that it can't be used. I am back home.

Three hours later I see my parents. They expect a young, refreshed face – free, proud – and I try to have one for them.

It is strange coming back like this, of your own free will, to the chains of sumūd. Doesn't it make the Israelis wonder? Maybe it does, and that is why they are turning to shooting. We are too stubborn to be put off by mere humiliation. How will they get rid of us?

June 5

We were warned, of course, but we waited. After the fedayeen killed settlers in Hebron, the Israelis said: 'Wait until the thirty days of mourning are over. We shall avenge our brothers' deaths. Two eyes for an eye.' We waited. That is the role of samidīn, to stay put. On June 2, precisely thirty days after the Hebron shooting, there were attempts to assassinate three of our mayors and a bomb went off in the crowded Hebron market, wounding eight samidīn.

At 8 a.m., bombs exploded in the cars of Ramallah Mayor Karim Khalaf and Nablus Mayor Bassam Shaka'a, as they started the engines of their cars on their way to work. Khalaf lost one leg, Shaka'a lost both. Ibrahim Tawil, Mayor of El-Bireh, left home late that day. Friends told him about Khalaf's and Shaka'a's bombs, so he did not touch his car. Later in the day, a Druse army sapper was seriously wounded when trying to defuse the bomb. The bombs in Hebron also went off at about 8 a.m.

The fedayeen, who thirty days ago stood on a Hebron rooftop

and fired at the Israeli settlers, escaped to freedom.* The samidīn on whose rooftop they stood had their house demolished by the Israeli army – without being able to boast of having done anything to deserve the punishment.

The fedayeen, who said to hell with everything, are somewhere across the river, running free and proud. All of Hebron's samidīn are locked up under a month-long curfew, at the mercy of rampaging soldiers. During house-to-house searches, the Hebronites were made to crawl on all fours and say, 'I am an animal'; children were forced at gunpoint to spit in their parents' faces.

The fedayeen, whose pride and dignity are intact, are sitting somewhere around a campfire discussing military tactics. They speak the language of the soldiers and meet the Israelis on equal terms. We, all West Bank samidīn, sit waiting for the thirty days to pass, waiting for the machine guns to start chopping. Waiting, defenceless, as in a slaughterhouse, for our turn to come.

So much is clear; these are indisputable facts. No less clear is the policy behind the creation of these facts. Fear, shame and humiliation are supposed to drive us samidīn into denouncing the fedayeen and into renouncing our sumūd. The Israelis think they can force the following choice on us: relinquishing our sumūd by physically leaving our land – exile; or mentally relinquishing our sumūd by staying and collaborating with the occupiers.

I have only this to say to them: I can see very clearly what you are up to; one hardly needs a subtle intellect for that. This is my answer. Your tactics only make the thought of collaborating with you more hateful than ever. And I will never leave this land.

As to the fedayeen: the reason I don't join them is that I have a job to do here as Sāmid. They and I are fighting for the same thing. I admit that I am very afraid. I admit that I am

*They were caught in September 1980 and sentenced to life imprisonment on July 5, 1981.

57

confused. I admit that I envy the fedayeen their freedom and their self-pride. You may have all that, but you won't have me; you won't have me condemning the fedayeen; and you won't have my land without me. I know no more now than this: I am Sāmid and you won't get what you want out of me.

Summer, 1980

Fear

When I left Manara Square there were still a few lights on and one or two people about. Driving away, towards home, I felt the light go out behind me. I stopped off at a shop that was just about to close and, as I left, the shopkeeper dimmed his lights. I drove on and the lights ahead of me also began to go off, one by one, until everything was dark.

The world was a pitch-black hole – no houses, no people, no hills, no valleys. An injured cat streaked across the road under my headlights, and I barely avoided killing it. As I reached the turning to my street, there was a sudden glare from the headlights of an army jeep parked two houses away from mine. I continued driving down the main road, parked about a hundred metres away, and walked back home. The jeep's lights had been switched off. The soldiers were talking through walkie-talkies – I couldn't make out what they were saying. I slunk in through my kitchen door. At first I thought of sitting in darkness. But I could not, and anyway they must have seen me. I turned on the lights and waited for them to come and take me away.

I waited for an hour, and then they drove off.

After they left, my neighbour Hani knocked on the door. 'Did they ask about me?' he whispered.

'No,' I said, and he limped off. I heard his mother locking their doors.

Only now do I understand, really understand, why she will not pursue the investigation of the shooting – why she will not file charges against the army. She lives in fear of the soldiers knocking at night and taking Hani away. I have heard so many stories of people who have this fear, but only now has it become mine as well. For they do it to writers too. They found Kamal Nasir in his room in Beirut and shot him. Three times, in the mouth. Newspaper editors and university teachers – hauled out of their beds at midnight, and held for days, for months.

As a lawyer I have heard much about how they interrogate, about torture that cannot be proved when the prisoner finally comes out. You hear all these stories during the day, nod your head, are perhaps horrified, but in the sanity of broad daylight they are detached – something to talk about and act against. It is at night, in dreams, that this accumulative information lashes out, and you wake up screaming with nightmares. It is this fear that no one acknowledges . . . no one talks about.

I have seen fear all around me. People afraid of being dragged out in the middle of the night for interrogation, afraid of waking up one morning to find themselves banished to another land across the border; afraid of waking up in a tent outside their demolished home. Some people take a different route to work every day for fear of being arrested.

As a rational lawyer, you try to work out which fears are justified, with some correspondence to reality. But you cannot tell any more, and what does it matter? These fears govern your behaviour, and who can tell when a rational fear becomes paranoia or, worse, insanity?

Once, my own fears were confined to nightmares. Now they have invaded my waking hours. Since going to Geneva, every soldier I see, I fear. I wish the book* were already published. It is the waiting that is worse than anything.

Tonight, waiting for the soldiers, I had one of those strange daydreams that take complete possession of you – a waking nightmare.

The soldiers burst into my room and as they surrounded

**The West Bank and the Rule of Law.*

me their uniforms faded away and turned into striped rags, and their cheeks and their eyes hollowed out and their guns dissolved. They bared their arms and on each one was a concentration camp number. They surrounded me in a tight circle, pointing their tattooed arms at me. As they stood there, all their flesh withered away, and they were just skeletons, interlocked skeletons, gripping each other, encircling me.

'Your turn has come,' they whispered.

'Why? What have I done?'

'You are Sāmid. We know all about you, we have been watching you. No one, let that be known, no one will ever get away from us. We are the survivors of our six million brothers.

'We are here on earth to avenge our brothers' deaths. This time we shall exterminate every one, before they get a chance to touch us.'

'But what have I done?'

'What have you done? Don't look so innocent.

'You seek our destruction – as does everyone. You, the Arabs, are the new Nazis. But we shall get you first. Never Again. Remember what we did to Kamal Nasir. You cannot hide. Remember what we say. Never Again. Never Again. Never Again.'

As their voices faded out, one reached out and stamped my arm with a number. And then they were gone.

I do not know how long I was sitting before I heard the jeep drive away. And then Hani knocked.

I have always had fears: fear of losing myself here, fear of succumbing to despair, fear of being blinded by hate. Fear of the end, of the blood at the end, fear of what they plan for us.

But since the book, I have lost control of my fears and they have become specific and hard. My stomach contracts. I know my fears are crazy. But so are my enemies. Once I could say that this or that about Begin, Levinger, all the Gush Emunim people, is insane. But now their insanity has infected me. What do they mean when they say 'Never again', when they say night and day that everyone is a Nazi and that they will never again let the world get them?

Sometimes, I think I am the victim of the victims of the Nazis. Fate has decreed that I also pay the price of the holocaust; fate – through nightmares, through the great subconscious – has decreed that I inherit the memory, the fear and the horror of Auschwitz.

This is one of the biggest changes since Begin came to power. Once, in the old Labour Party days, we were surrounded by supermen. They did not see themselves as victims of the holocaust – on the contrary, they saw themselves and acted as the liberated, new Jews. I was more sane then in my fears. My fear then was that their superiority would outwit and defeat me. But now, now – my fear has become as demented as are my oppressors. I have the horrible suspicion that I am more aware of the concentration camps, think about them more and dream about them more than the average Israeli of my age does. He acts, and I dream the dreams that he should have. If he had my dreams, he would be as paralysed as I am.

I wish that the book were published and that they would come and take me away. I have begun to look forward to physical torture to end this nightmare of waiting. But as I write, it suddenly occurs to me that they will not do anything. That they know my fears as they know everything about all of us. That they will leave me like this and won't say a word. Leave me to go mad – for they have different ways of dealing with different people.

The nights – it is the nights I hate. Alone, with no one to divert you, no action to occupy you, and nothing to protect you. So I write and I write and I write. And soon morning will come. Daylight and sanity. I will go to the office, talk in my capacity as a lawyer to the military governors and civilian colonizers – run around pretending that it's all in a day's work, which it is – and put off till nightfall the reign of terror.

The Gentle Ones

Today, a most polite and soft-spoken soldier stopped me at a road-block. He addressed me in Arabic and gently asked me for my identity card. I could not but bid him farewell with a warm and genuine smile that hid no curse.

His gentle presence started me thinking about the double face we samidīn have acquired through the years of living as an occupied people. We have learned to fake a smile while cursing between our teeth – the duplicity of the weak.

I thought, also, of this gentle soldier and others of his kind in Israel. For I know that they exist, even if they are few. He might be totally against the occupation, perhaps is even a pacifist deep down. If I have to do it, he may have said to himself, the least I can do is try to be human, work from within to lessen the evil, until I complete my military service, or my reserve duty.

The friendly soldier at the road-block was a solitary soul, surrounded by the usual bullies who seemed to exaggerate their crass conduct in order to counterbalance his politeness – perhaps afraid that we Arabs might get the wrong idea.

And as I thought of him I felt rising anger: it seemed very wrong that this kind of peace-seeker should try to dispel his discomfort over the occupation by assuming a gentle attitude. Doesn't he see that, together with thousands of other reservists, he is an agent of a policy with definite aims and objectives and that he is helping to implement it, whether he likes it or not? Surely he must see this. It is hard not to think that he is trying to have the best of both worlds – actively participating in our oppression but smiling apologetically as he does it, seeking to be liked, despite it. We have been told so many times about Israeli democracy. Does this not impose on such people some responsibilities? They cannot treat their role as a matter of unavoidable fate.

But am I being fair? True, a Jew can get away with saying

much more than an Arab, without getting thrown into jail. He would never be banished. But the psychological pressures are great. He is treated as a traitor to the Zionist cause. And if he actually refused to go into the army, he would find himself in jail. And how free is someone, who has to work and to provide for his family, to devote himself to political activity? These are unrealistic demands that I hurl at him.

But this goes much deeper: underlying my anger and demands is an idealistic belief in the rationality of a democratic society – that these gentle souls would succeed by persuasion to reverse policies. This seems to be increasingly untrue of Israel. And when I hear an Israeli friend say that he has been called up for reserve duty and see the despair, almost that of a prisoner, on his face – I feel deep fear, and despair of my own.

For it is at moments such as these that I feel both how deeply ingrained and how unjustified is my faith, my blind faith in the power of reason. Whence comes the idea, which guides everything I do and hope for, that if Israelis knew more of what is happening here they would act to prevent the evil? True, there is much ignorance, but this must be at least partly a result of indifference. And those who feel the evil are not necessarily those who have much information, and feeling isn't acting anyway – it just as easily leads to silent despair. And many of the worst are those who know the most – they are the initiators and perpetuators of our oppression.

And this much is certainly clear: these gentle soldiers who hate the occupation, when the day comes they will follow their leaders' call to war, just as now they don their uniforms to be part of the occupying reserve forces. There is no question as to which direction their bullets will fly in, when the order is given.

As I write now, I feel robbed of my anger at the gentle soldier. He is no less a puppet of fate than I – with no mastery over his own destiny – nothing but putty in the hands of policy-makers and army generals. That is the ugly truth about him and me.

The Shooting of Hani

Two months have gone by since my fifteen-year-old neighbour Hani was shot in his left leg by an Israeli soldier. He spent three weeks in hospital and underwent several operations. Today, he had his fifth, and more will be needed. His leg is still in very bad shape. I want to write the report of how it happened: the Israeli army, I can see, is paving the way to wiping it from the records. I am all too familiar with the procedures for doing this, as a lawyer, as Sāmid, from the countless other cases in which this has been done. Soon the shooting will be forgotten by everybody but Hani, his mother and a few close friends. Even if a trial were to be held now, the confusion of the witnesses would make it easy meat for the defence. But the army need not worry about a trial. It has been made all too clear to Um Hani that if she files charges, her son will be charged for participating in the demonstration against Kahane in April. This could mean a long jail-term with his smashed, infected leg. She has also heard many stories about the harassment of people who do dare file charges against the army or any other Jewish institution on the West Bank. Everyone has heard these stories, and fewer and fewer people are filing charges. Um Hani is adamant: she will not seek redress.

Why do I bother to write this story down, when there are so many others that I have heard and left at that? Because something Um Hani said has stuck in my mind. She said: 'What does it matter?' when I suggested filing charges against the army. 'What difference does it make?' she asked. 'Just keep those monsters out of my life.'

In her, I see how anger has gradually, through the years of occupation, given way to despair. Anger fuels memory, keeps it alive. Without this fuel, you give up even the right to assert the truth. You let others write your history for you, and this is the ultimate capitulation. We samidīn cannot fight the Israelis' brute physical force but we must keep the anger burning – steel our wills to fight the lies. It is up to us to remember and record.

Um Hani's defeat frightens me because she is not easily intimidated. It is not mere physical fear of soldiers that has deterred her – she is used to that: her husband, who died several years ago, was a Communist and spent his time in and out of jails. For years she had been very familiar with harassment by soldiers. It is not the soldiers *alone* who have defeated her. It is her feeling that there is no one but the soldiers, no one to appeal to against them. If you ask Um Hani now about the event, she will hardly mention the soldier. She will tell you only about the treatment her son received at the Israeli hospital in Jerusalem. It was that, the feeling that there too he was in enemy hands, that finally broke her, although this has been gradually led up to via a series of incidents. She is used to separating the army from the people. Soldiers are soldiers anywhere. In fact the Israeli soldiers used to be kinder than those others she had been accustomed to, although this is no longer true. But now she believes that they represent the attitude of all Israelis. She has given up, she doesn't care about what really happened, how it happened, she just wants to protect her son; to keep the monsters – by which she by now means all the Israelis – out of her life.

You can be frightened by external forces into keeping the truth to yourself: keeping it and – through anger – remembering it. But if you no longer care about it, you forget; and you may as well collaborate and not suffer physically. Paradoxically, it is hardest to be coldly angry and accurate on behalf of those you are closest to. You feel their pain and sorrow and care less about facts. But if my sumūd as a lawyer is to mean anything, I must at least be able to tell my people's stories. Of course, I will not urge Um Hani to file charges. I would not jeopardize Hani, any more than I would insist that a client assert that he was tortured if this would greatly harm his case. But I fear that I am letting go: expecting nothing of others, or of myself. I am beginning to be wearied by the constant attrition of not being believed. As a lawyer I have to rely, almost always, on frightened, confused and often conflicting memories as my sole evidence against the meticulously documented version of the Israeli authorities. I know very well how much goodwill and patience are needed to piece together and believe the accounts I rely on. I know it is naïve to expect this goodwill even from objective judges. I know very well the psychological mechanism that makes people believe the concise, documented account as opposed to the confused, incoherent, verbal one. I know this all so well that I sometimes feel that it is ludicrous, irrational, to expect anyone to believe the story of the weak. There is a cumulative attrition of collective experience working here as well; all the Palestinian villages that have been wiped from the face of the earth – all the land records that have been lost – and you getting up and telling the world what you know and not being able to prove it; being told that, of course we understand your feelings, but aren't you exaggerating, letting your emotions carry you away?

This is often said in kindness, not by people who have any interest in denying your version. Not by the officials whose story you are contesting, but by kindly disposed, even concerned individuals and institutions. Kindly – but firmly you are not believed. Somehow, it is this that undermines me more than anything – because it deprives me even of the anger of the contest.

So I am writing Hani's story, for the record; and for Hani and his mother. It is one of many thousands of stories that should at least have been documented.

On the day of Kahane's insolent visit to Ramallah, Hani was at home with his mother because his school was on strike. Since her husband's death, Um Hani has brought up her two children virtually on her own, which demands much courage and independence in this male-dominated society. Her elder son is in university in the States, doing brilliantly, and it is her hard-earned money that got him there. Now she lives with just Hani, and it is heartwarming to see the care they take of each other.

Although Um Hani loved her husband very much and is not bitter about the life she led because of his political commitments, she has become determined to keep Hani out of politics. It is difficult now, when the schoolchildren often seem to be carrying the flag of resistance in the occupied territories. She had been afraid for some time that Hani would follow its call.

Hani was excited by the demonstration against Kahane in Manara Square on April 28. Friends came to tell him about it, and urged him to join them. His mother wouldn't let him and Hani stayed at home. He is considerate in a manner rare in teenagers, and would never do anything he thought would upset his mother.

She finally let him go out to buy meat. The next time she saw him was hours later, in hospital, with his leg in shreds.

Hani says that as he was approaching the butcher's he heard shouts and saw several men run into the alley, pursued by two soldiers. The army had begun to disperse the demonstration, and people were fleeing through Ramallah's tiny side-streets. The soldiers were firing – one may assume, in the air this time, as Hani was the only gunfire casualty in Ramallah that day. Hani turned on his heels and ran with the crowds. He took a turning towards home and heard someone running after him. He turned his head and saw a soldier. Hani reached a friend's yard and jumped over the low fence. He heard the soldier shout at him to stop running and to put his hands up. He did, with his back to the voice. He heard a shot and fell to the ground, bleeding from his left leg.

Then a soldier was standing over him, shouting down into his face: 'You were hurt when you jumped from a moving car. You and some others were driving around Ramallah, throwing stones and petrol bombs at soldiers. You were hurt when you fell – understand?'

Hani says he was too astounded and in too much shock and pain to feel frightened. Lying on his back, looking up at the soldier who was aiming his gun down at him, he said 'That's not true.'

The soldier began kicking him, repeating the story. Hani thinks that he blacked out. The next thing he saw was his friend's father coming out of the house and the soldier running off.

Abu-Fu'ad bandaged Hani's leg with his shirt. Another neighbour had meanwhile called an ambulance. I have spoken to both of them: they both say that they heard the shot and saw Hani falling, and then saw a soldier standing over him. Neither actually saw the soldier fire.

When the ambulance arrived from Ramallah Hospital, an army jeep would not let it take Hani. An officer said that Hani must first be taken for questioning to the military headquarters. Salim, the doctor who had come in the ambulance, was a friend of Um Hani's. He wanted to give Hani first aid. But the officer said that they would be reaching the hospital very shortly and that it could wait until then.

Hani was taken to the headquarters, where he spent over an hour being questioned about his role in the demonstration. There, too, he was told repeatedly that he had been throwing petrol bombs at soldiers, and they threatened him with imprisonment. Hani was too weak to remember much more of the interrogation. They bundled him on to a jeep which began driving around Ramallah, looking for trouble-makers.

The jeep finally took him to Ramallah Hospital. Salim had collected Hani's mother from work and the two of them had been waiting at the hospital for three hours. Salim wanted to rush Hani to the operating table. The soldier said that Hani could not be treated in Ramallah and must be taken to the Hadassah Hospital in Jerusalem and be treated there. Salim blocked the exit to the hospital with his car and insisted on administering first aid. Hani's mother begged the soldiers to let her son be treated here. She told them she could never afford the fees for Hadassah. The officer promised that the military government would foot the bill.

The Ramallah ambulance set off for Jerusalem. Hani's mother rode in the back with her son. When they reached the Hadassah extension on Mount Scopus, Hani was not allowed into the emergency room. The doctor told Um Hani that 'there is no room'. They continued their journey across Jerusalem to the Hadassah branch in Ein Kerem, at the opposite end of town. Hani was continually losing and regaining consciousness. Seven hours after he was shot, he was finally admitted into hospital, in Ein Kerem, and given treatment. He was there for three weeks, was finally released, and then underwent two more operations. In Hadassah, where each operation was conducted by a different house surgeon, they said that they could not set the bone right. Hani's bone was smashed, his muscles and nerves torn to shreds. As far as I have understood, the medical reports confirm that the cause of his wound was a dum-dum bullet.

After Hani had been in hospital for a week, the hospital demanded payment. Um Hani replied that the military government had said that it would pay. The hospital said that it knew of no such arrangement. When she tried to get confirmation of the promise from the military headquarters, she was told that they had never heard of Hani – that there was no reason for the army to pay for Hani's treatment, since the army was not responsible for his injury. Hani was let out after three weeks. Um Hani had to borrow vast sums to pay for his hospitalization in Hadassah.

Three days after Hani was admitted, two officers from the military police turned up at the hospital to question him. Hani says that they asked detailed questions about the shooting. They kept on returning to the point that Hani did not actually see the person who shot him, and suggested it may have been another demonstrator. The story that he fell from a car was no longer mentioned, but they made it clear to Hani that he would be put on trial for his part in the demonstration. They would hear nothing of his claim that he got caught up in it by mistake.

The following day, three soldiers came to the yard in which Hani was shot. They combed the ground and interviewed the neighbours. Here, too, they returned to the point that neither had actually *seen* the soldier shoot: they just heard the soldier shout at Hani to put his hands up, heard a shot, and saw Hani on the ground – with a soldier standing over him. Since then, nothing has been heard from the military authorities.

I only visited Hani once in hospital. The first time I was let in without difficulty. The second time, when I asked to see him, I was told that there was no patient by that name in the hospital. When I insisted, the duty nurse took out a list and said she was sorry but Hani was not allowed visitors. After several days, everyone – except Hani's mother and uncle – who tried to visit him got the same reply. One nurse mumbled something once about 'security reasons'.

If you ask Um Hani now about the event you will probably get a rather muddled account of how it happened. She doesn't care. Ask her if she will file charges and she will look at you with something akin to hate; you are suggesting that her son suffer more. What you will hear most about is the treatment in Hadassah. More than the shooting itself, and the distortion of justice, what pains her and preoccupies her is the treatment Hani received in Hadassah. She said that she felt they were in enemy hands. I wondered whether this was not the exaggeration of a worried mother. Hadassah is famous for its treatment of Arab patients from all over the world. But on the one occasion I was allowed in, I saw what she meant. The hostility and coldness were marked. Hani's calls went unanswered and nurses did not bother to conceal their animosity. It became worse, Um Hani said, after the May 2 shooting at Hebron. When the Jewish wounded were brought in, she literally feared for Hani's life: there was an atmosphere of war in the ward. Um Hani spent every day in the hospital, taking the long bus-ride early in the morning and late at night, bringing food with her. Hani would be left unfed for whole days on end. When he would ask why, he was told that they thought they were going to operate. Hani laughs: 'If they operated on me as often as they starved me, they'd have no time for anyone else.'

I said I fear defeat because we are losing anger. But perhaps, if we can still laugh, we are all right. And we do – laugh – even if it is bitter.

Maha

Today I visited Rosie and she told me for the first time the story of her 'baby sister', Maha, who has served three years of her twelve-year prison sentence.

Maha was four when the occupation began. Unlike my generation, she had no complicated adjustments to make. Enemy soldiers patrolling her town were a fact of life she grew up with. Her parents and elder brother and sister did have to adjust, however, and would talk freely about their hatred for the occupier without thinking about the mark this left on the child.

She was a good, quiet girl. She went to school and never talked politics. She was not known to take part in any of the demonstrations, tyre-burning and other forms of teenage resistance to the occupation. She was serious, a bit withdrawn, and her father used to think: 'At least for her I won't have to plead with the military governor for mercy.'

One night, three years ago, when Maha was sixteen, there was a violent knocking at her parents' door. Soldiers burst into the house, guns aimed, and shouted: 'Where is Maha?' She came out of her room quietly, showing no signs of resistance or surprise. The soldiers surrounded her, handcuffed her and pushed her out of the door and on to a jeep. Her parents' stunned question: 'Why, why, what has she done?' went unanswered that night. It remained unanswered for three months. For three months they knocked on every legal and military door they could think of, and no one would tell them where Maha was. No one even admitted to knowing who she was.

But there were unofficial rumours. They heard that Maha was suspected of planting bombs in Jerusalem. They had cheered when they saw buildings damaged on television. It was not real to them – the fedayeen keeping up the spirit of resistance. They found no way of connecting this, in their minds, with Maha. It could not be. She was such a quiet, bashful girl. When could she have gone to Jerusalem? She went to school every day and came straight home. They did not believe the rumours, they were too incredible. Her father spent his days waiting at officials' doors, asking neighbours, relatives in other towns, schoolfriends. He stopped working, and in the nights neither he nor his wife could sleep.

About three months after Maha was taken, her father was walking aimlessly near the main square when someone rushed up to him and screamed: 'I have seen Maha. She is in an army jeep with handcuffed prisoners.' He pointed in the direction that the jeep had taken, and her father ran and ran, knocking down people, panting, dizzy. He saw the jeep. The soldiers had stopped to buy something in a shop. He reached it in time to see his Maha lying on the floor. A woman soldier and some men soldiers were using her and other prisoners as a foot rest. Her father reached up into the jeep: 'My darling!' The soldiers shouted something at him, but his determination must have stopped them. 'Father, I am cold. Give me something to warm my body,' was all she said. Her father pulled off his coat and managed to throw it over her, his hand skimming her thin face, before the jeep drove away.

Now he could find out. Now they would tell him. Maha was being transferred from the interrogation headquarters in the Russian Compound in Jerusalem – where she had confessed to a series of bomb plantings – to the Ramallah prison to await trial. After her confessions were made and the charge-sheet drawn, her family was allowed to visit her. 'Is it true, my daughter?' her father pleaded. 'Yes, father. It is true. I am a fida'iyyeh,'* she answered quietly, but with pride and confidence. His baby Maha.

She pleaded not guilty at the trial but admitted proudly to all the facts. The lawyer could do nothing to dissuade little Maha. She was convicted but, because of her age, was sentenced to only twelve years in prison. She might have got less, but her attitude in court did not elicit leniency. At one stage, when the judge told her to sit up straight and not to act so insolently, she stood up and shouted, 'You' – sweeping her hand across the courtroom – 'are all scum and not worth the soles of my shoes. I am a fida'iyyeh and I do not care what you decide to do with me!'

At the trial, her parents learned about their quiet daughter's activities. The fedayeen would collect her between classes and, in her free time – there was plenty with the schools so often on strike – they would drive her to various places, amongst them Jerusalem. In her innocent, quiet manner, wearing her school uniform, she would carry the bomb in her school bag and place it where they told her. Her parents do remember that once, when they were visiting relatives in Jordan, she disappeared for the whole day. She said later that she had been with friends. They believe that is when she was recruited. They, her brother and her sister still cannot understand how it happened – how she grew up so different from them.

They visit Maha in jail and sometimes she slips them a message on rolled-up pieces of paper, transferred from mouth to mouth as they kiss. On one such message she told how two lesbians were put in her cell at night and she woke up screaming. Other stories about her come from released prisoners. One woman prisoner told how once, when she was sweeping the dining-room floor, the guard kicked her and called her a 'filthy whore'. Maha got up, turned the table over and said to

*Freedom fighter, feminine form of fida'i.

the soldier: 'You are a whore. This woman you are kicking is a freedom fighter! You are not worthy of sweeping the floor she walks on!' She went on cursing and screaming, and she was finally handcuffed and dragged away by the soldiers. Her punishment was several months of solitary confinement.

Her sister cannot say where Maha learned this language, where she got the courage. Did she identify with the pictures showing Palestinian youths in camps in Lebanon, proudly carrying arms and training for battle? Although they are baffled, Rosie said, they cannot but be proud when they pay her visits in jail and hear stories of how she encourages the other prisoners. Maha, Rosie said, has more faith, more determination and more courage than all of us.

Maha is not the only Sāmdeh-turned-fida'iyyeh in prison. She is with thousands of teenagers and men and women, most of them young when the occupation began. No one knows exactly how and when they learned to become freedom fighters – but their number is constantly and rapidly growing.

Kamil, Another Sāmid

'Could I ask you a favour?' Kamil shouted, running up to my car as I picked my way through a maze of earthen-brick houses in Jericho. 'We are waiting for the *khityara*,'* he said. 'She has gone to visit my sister near the mosque and she has not returned. She must be here for something important and she hasn't shown up yet. Can I ask you to drive me to her to bring her back here?'

*Kamil was referring to his mother. *Khityara* is the feminine form of the word meaning 'old person'. It is in common use for 'parent' amongst village people.

'I have to stop to see some friends for a few minutes, can you wait?'

'No. I am sorry. You see, she must be here before sundown. Could you please do me this favour? We have prepared everything and she hasn't come.'

'All right. Come on.'

Kamil shooed away the chickens and ducks surrounding him, climbed into the car, and told his daughters to go inside to their mother. We rode off together.

'You remember my cousin? The one who was walking with my sister when you saw us on this road last week? It's for him that we need my mother.'

'Why? What's the matter with him?'

'You see, he and my sister have been married for four months now and he still has not slept with her.'

'Why not?'

'His penis won't rise. We have tried everything. Everything they told us to do, we have done. We rubbed his penis with hot oil, we gave him a massage, we brought the *Haj* to drive evil spirits away, the Qadi himself prayed over his head. But nothing has worked so far.'

'Maybe there is something physically wrong with him? How was he before he married?'

'He says it used to rise, but now he has no desire. He's very unhappy and threatens to do all sorts of things to himself. I tell him: if you do, you will only lose yourself. Nobody will care about you any more.' Kamil sighed. 'I don't know. It's God's will. Just like this occupation.'

'So what are you going to do about it? Did anyone examine him?'

'I looked at him, and I think it looks strange. It is very big and his balls are huge. He says he had desire before, but not any more, and it won't rise. My poor sister.'

Kamil was silent, then said, 'You know, I think it is really because he cannot talk to her. A woman needs to be played with, laughed with, humoured. He just cannot talk, he doesn't know how to act, even though he is already sixteen.'

'And how old is she?'

'Fourteen.'

'What a tragedy . . . What are you planning to do tonight?'

'A friend of ours had a dream several nights ago. A sheikh appeared to him in the dream and told him to come and tell us what we should do. Like this: fill up a large tub with water and put four kilos of salt in it. Let him immerse three-quarters of his body in the water and put all kinds of incense in the house, and then let the couple sleep together. All this has to be performed before sundown. The *khityara* is the expert, and she told me to prepare everything and not to begin until she comes. Sundown is close now, but she isn't here.'

We found Um Kamil helping her daughter with her ten children in her shack near the mosque. The *khityara* got into the car and recited a verse from the Qur'an invoking God's protection for this ride.

Kamil explained why she did this. They had lost Ahmad (whom he called 'our jewel'). He was a truck-driver taking vegetables across the Allenby Bridge to Amman. A few days before, he had veered off the road to avoid an approaching car, and hit a wall. The steering wheel had pressed against his chest, suffocating him to death. This is his fate, Kamil explained: thus it was 'written' – that he should die.

'I must make sure there are no evil spirits in the house,' Kamil's mother said. 'I will check everything carefully. Did you bring enough salt?'

'Yes,' said Kamil, 'and I have already put it in the water.'

'My unlucky daughters. They had bad luck, all of them,' Um Kamil muttered to herself. Then she turned to Kamil and said: 'Your little sister, Zayna, has been thrown out of the house by Muhammad. He blames her for letting the neighbours' boys play football in their yard. She had nothing to do with it. But he told her to give him the key and go. And now this. Poor Zayna.'

'God will look after them,' Kamil and I said in unison.

'God be with us,' said Um Kamil. 'Have we enough incense?'

'Yes.'

As we were approaching the house, the *khityara* asked: 'What shall we do if this doesn't work?'

'Let him go home. We shall have done everything we could.'

'May God be merciful,' Um Kamil muttered.

'It is written like this, *Yamma*.* It is God's will, everything has to happen his way.' Then Kamil turned to me and continued: 'It's just like this occupation we are under. It is God's will. When God changes his mind, the Jews will go. When He changes his mind, Khalil's penis will rise.'

I dropped Kamil and his mother at the house and said: 'May it be God's will that things be different.'

Kamil and his mother walked briskly towards the house. As I was driving away I caught a glimpse of Khalil and his bride. He looked young and delicate. She had the charm and radiance of a fourteen-year-old girl. The house was lit up and looked festive. If it works tonight, it will be like a wedding night and they will wave the red handkerchief with pride and be festive all night. If it doesn't, perhaps God will send another emissary to give them yet another hint as to what must be done. They will continue to be like most of us – waiting for God's anger to be appeased.

The Grave

We went to visit a grave – Enoch and I – a grave marked with a large, flat stone without inscription. We seized on a day we were both free and packed up a picnic bag and set off on our

*Colloquial for 'mother'.

expedition. This was no grand, historic tour of Old Jaffa, but sheer romanticism. I had heard the story of the grave not long ago and was enchanted by it. And Enoch is the best person for this kind of outing.

The grave we sought was that of a much-loved and very successful doctor in the Jaffa of the old days. His widow had visited us recently in Ramallah, and her story was fresh in my mind. The doctor had died quite suddenly, at the height of his career in the early 1940s, after examining a woman with a fatal disease. The infection, his widow said, was transmitted from the woman's mouth through a cut in his hand. He died three days after touching her, as antibiotics had not yet reached Palestine. His last wishes as he lay dying were that his young wife would promise to educate the children, making sure they lacked for nothing, and that she would take care of the hospital.

His widow told us that she cried for seven days and then dried her tears and dedicated her life to the fulfilment of her promise to him. One thing she insisted on: her husband must be buried in the garden, under her bedroom window. At night she would draw comfort from the thought of him buried under the tree that they both loved.

She wanted to build him the most beautiful tomb in Palestine. Masons came, and stone experts, but nothing they suggested satisfied her dreams. The years flew by, she was kept busy with the children and the hospital, and still she waited for the right idea for the tombstone. It had to be perfect, and in the meantime she had much to do.

When the 1948 war broke out, she fled Jaffa, leaving behind the grave still unmarked. She travelled through many lands until she settled in England, where she continued to fulfil her promise to give the children the best of everything. But for all her dedication, she herself was unfulfilled: her husband's grave was without a tombstone.

One morning, soon after she came to Ramallah, she put on a long, black veil and went to Jaffa. We had arranged for a Hebrew-speaking Arab from Jaffa to accompany her on her visit to her old home and her husband's grave. When she returned in the evening she said that she must speak to me urgently. She wanted to know: would the Israelis let her put up a tombstone on her husband's grave? I doubted whether they would but, not wanting to discourage her, I said, honestly, that it was worth a try. I told her that I would very much like to see the grave myself. She seemed very gratified, but her face fell into sadness again as she described her dismay at how run-down the place looked. It had become an Israeli government maternity hospital – but that was not what bothered her; in fact, she was glad it was still a hospital. What upset her were the unkempt gardens and peeling paint. And she noticed that one of the stone lions flanking the steps to their house was broken. I was surprised that she asked no questions about the possibility of compensation and reclaiming some of the property – but her mind was apparently taken up with one thing: her hope that she would be allowed to build her tombstone.

It was this grave that we set out to visit, Enoch and I. The widow had given us complicated instructions and I had drawn a map of the grounds which I had in my pocket.

We felt rather tense as we entered the main building. We had forgotten it was inhabited and had somehow imagined we would have the place to ourselves. There were many doctors and nurses about, and there was a general bustle of efficiency and authority.

We walked through quickly, out into the main grounds at the back. I took out the drawing and we began to look for the grave. There were several small buildings dotted around the grounds: one of them must be the doctor's home. We walked over to a tree that seemed to be right and began scraping at the dry weeds underneath with our feet. It did not seem to be there. Enoch climbed up on to a wall to see what he could see from there.

As I was waiting for him to come down I felt a tap on my

shoulder. I turned to find what was clearly some security officer. And indeed he asked me for my identity papers and ordered Enoch off the wall and asked him for his.

'What are you doing here?' he asked. 'You can't hang about here like that.'

I felt a ridiculous urge to lie – to say that it was my father's grave I was looking for. But I stuck to the truth. The man listened to my mumbled explanation suspiciously. He ordered us to wait and said he would make inquiries.

Enoch and I sat down on a bench. It was only then I noticed that the grounds were full of babies and young mothers. It seemed strange, suddenly, looking for a grave where births take place.

The man returned. 'There is no grave here!' he said. This was the unmistakable ring of authority that has the power to assert and deny the truth. 'Get a move on,' he continued.

Enoch and I stood rooted to the ground. The guard started to push us and then I heard someone saying: 'Hey, what's going on here?'

A smiling man came up and looked at us kindly, obviously ready to help. He stood over us, waiting for an explanation. The guard had relaxed his grip. I looked up at the kind intruder and then at the guard – the two faces of authority, the friendly and the hostile – waiting for an answer, a proof, evidence.

I looked at Enoch and saw that he agreed that we should leave. I was not going to give them the pleasure of either granting or denying me the right to believe the grave was there. Enoch didn't need a proof from me. I was not alone.

Enoch and I turned away and walked towards the main building without answering the kind authority's question. We continued into the bustling street. Neither of us spoke. We went to the beach and had our picnic in silence.

Just once, Enoch spoke: 'We were looking on the wrong side, you know.'

I took out the drawing and saw that he was right. We would have found it if they had left us alone.

Pornography

Abu-'Isa lives in Batn el-Hawa (the Belly of the Wind). This is the section in Ramallah that connects Hārat Dār Ibrahim* with the Ramallah–Latrun road. It was given this name because it is the windiest part of our town, so windy you can be swept from your feet when the winter gales are blowing.

The wind blowing through Batn el-Hawa comes from the coast. Standing on this street and looking west, you see the chains of hills like interlocking fingers lacing their way down towards the sea. From many places in hilly Ramallah you can see the wadis wending their way west, but from nowhere is their pattern as beautifully etched as from here, in this funnel of the winds – Batn el-Hawa.

Abu-'Isa inherited his land in Batn el-Hawa from his grandfather. He grew up on it in a shack, and ever since childhood had lived with the dream of one day building a stone house on it for all the extended family to live in together. Neither his grandfather nor his father could afford it. But Abu-'Isa was luckier. In his time the price of land soared. His neighbour, whose son made a fortune in Kuwait, kept coming down the rocky path to his shack – day in, day out – offering to buy part of it for a tempting price. At first Abu-'Isa was loath to part with even an inch. But his family talked him into selling enough to have money to begin building a house, and a dream, generations old, began to come to life.

It took a long time. First, stones were chosen from a special quarry, and then they were carried down to the plot where Abu-'Isa personally oversaw the chiselling by the masons. He knew what he wanted, no architect was needed (they are rarely used in Ramallah) and all the family took part in all the

---

*The Quarter of the House of Ibrahim. Ibrahim was one of the seven brothers who founded Ramallah. Earliest accounts put this at the beginning of the sixteenth century.

stages of construction. It took several years because there was not enough money. But his son began sending instalments from the Gulf, and at last the house, every stone and corner personally supervised by Abu-'Isa, was finished. Planting the garden and orchards began.

Ensconced as a private kingdom in the Belly of the Winds, Dar Abu-'Isa is lodged in the westernmost entrance to Ramallah. His sons and his grandchildren surrounding him, Abu-'Isa benignly rules over a self-contained world.

It was to Abu-'Isa that I took Robert Stone. He is an American Jewish writer whom I met once in New York, and like a lot. He rang up several days ago to say that he was in Tel Aviv staying with relatives, and we arranged for him to visit me here. We had a long day together. He was fascinating to me – although very knowledgeable about the Palestinian-Israeli conflict, there is a freshness in his comments and in his concern that is free of the polemical platitudes that we who live here are usually subjected to. We talked much about the land dispute. He said that he was baffled by the weakness of the Palestinian national rhetoric – it often seemed, he said, so shallow compared with the richness of the Jews' claims to this land. He wasn't arguing, trying to score a point of any kind, and I felt no resentment. It is something that I myself have been feeling – that somehow, something important about the way we samidīn live on our land is not brought out in the war of words waged between Jews and Palestinians. I tried to explain what was lacking but thought that Stone would understand better if I took him to see Abu-'Isa. Towards evening, we walked out to Batn el-Hawa and called on the old man and his family.

When Robert asked Abu-'Isa about politics, the old man had nothing to say. Nor did he seem to follow the answers that his son Bāsel gave about Palestinian leadership, a state, independence, etc. For Abu-'Isa has a state of his own. The only way he has ever referred to any government was as 'them', as opposed to us hill-dwellers. His home is quite literally his fortress, as are many other homes on the West Bank. They are the only security against governments that come and go, but always want taxes and have soldiers that sometimes raid the villages.

Only at one point was old Abu-'Isa drawn into talking about the Israelis. He said: 'I do not care who rules. They are all bad. They all want our money, and the Turks made our men join the army. But never before have we had a government that wanted to take our land from underneath our feet.' And he pointed a shaking finger at the bright lights of a Jewish settlement to the south.

When we left Abu-'Isa I felt a bit apologetic – the old man hadn't said very much. But Robert interrupted me excitedly and said that it was precisely Abu-'Isa's inarticulate, silent love that couldn't be relayed in any rhetoric, because he himself had no words for it. Robert used an analogy with pornography and love to explain what he meant. When you are exiled from your land, he said, you begin, like a pornographer, to think about it in symbols. You articulate your love for your land, in its absence, and in the process transform it into something else.

'We Jews had 2,000 years in which to become expert pornographers with a highly symbol-wrought, intellectualized yearning for this land – totally devoid of any memories or images of what it really looks like. And when Jews came to settle here this century, they saw the land through these symbols. Think of the almost mystical power that names of places here have for many Zionists,' Robert said. 'As for what it really looked like, they tried to transform it into the kinds of landscape they left in Europe.

'Perhaps second- and third-generation Israeli farmers have lost the pornographer's symbolism,' he continued, 'but the Gush Emunim people who are spilling on to the West Bank have renewed it – ranting and raving over every stick and stone in a land they never knew. It is like falling in love with an image of a woman, and then, when meeting her, being excited not by what is there but by what her image has come to signify for you. You stare at her, gloating, without really seeing her, let alone loving her.'

I have been thinking for some time about Robert's 'pornography'. He connects it with exile, and the longer it is, the richer the pornography. So, that makes me a very poor pornographer about the coast and Jaffa because, although I knew Jaffa only from stories, I grew up seeing its lights over the hills – and I had very strong visual images of what it had been like in my parents' days. Yet, when I see Jaffa now I do not gloat, I am sad. The Gush Emunim people are not only pornographers, but victorious possessors of the object of their imagination – and it is this victory that is essential for the gloating gleam in their eyes. Pornographers' symbols alone can't give you that.

But what about my feelings for Ramallah, the hills, the Jericho oasis? It is not true to say that I am like Abu-'Isa, tied for my security to a particular plot of land. I own no land. Still, there is a difference between the way I used to love the land around me and the way I do now.

Sometimes, when I am walking in the hills, say Batn el-Hawa – unselfconsciously enjoying the touch of the hard land under my feet, the smell of thyme and the hills and trees around me – I find myself looking at an olive tree, and as I am looking at it, it transforms itself before my eyes into a symbol of the samidīn, of our struggle, of our loss. And at that very moment, I am robbed of the tree; instead, there is a hollow space into which anger and pain flow.

I have often been baffled by this – the way the tree-turned-symbol is contrasted in my mind with the sight of red, newly turned soil, barbed wire, bulldozers tearing at the soft pastel hills – all the signs that a new Jewish settlement is in the making. This must be the beginning of pornography; the pains of a people have become my own personal, private ones. And the beauty of the hills and the olives have become symbols of my people. It is not *any* symbolism, but *national* symbolism that makes you into a land pornographer. It is the identification of the land with your people and through that with yourself. That is what the Gush Emunim people do – and it is their united aggression that has awoken in me or, rather, rammed into me the same kind of national possessiveness. And with it, the flip side of their gloating – the fury and the grief, and the image of an uprooted olive as a symbol of our oppression.

I have acquired my pornography for the West Bank through the experience of loss. And this is surely peculiar – having the feelings of an exile, a pornographer while still on your land? Maybe this is what the American Indians felt as the colonizers pushed them into reservations. But unlike the Indians, perhaps because of the speed of the takeover and because the area is so much smaller, we are learning fast. Before the occupation there was no national symbolism and cohesion specifically connected with the West Bank. The Israelis, I think, utilized this to the hilt when they came. What they probably don't realize is that we have learned their ways. Even Abu-'Isa, who always thought of himself and his house as a separate kingdom, is beginning, through the threat of an Israeli incursion, to extend his horizons. And his children and all of those growing up under occupation will grow into it naturally; for them the West Bank is theirs. All of it – personally theirs. Every settlement is a personal robbery.

Although I am glad that this is happening – we could not hope to fight off the Israelis without it – I cannot but allow myself a moment of anger and regret. I feel deep, deep resentment against this invasion of my innermost imagery and consciousness by the Israelis. As a child I took for granted a natural pleasure in this land – not a romantic love – my romantic vision was fastened on the magical lights of the inaccessible Jaffa. But since the occupation, I have begun to think of our hills as 'virginal', 'molested' by the Israeli bulldozers – the bulldozers that have for me become the symbol of the Israeli power over us. I am sure that my imagery would not be so replete with sexual-political symbols were I left to the privacy of my feelings. I can thank our occupiers, then, among other things, for instilling in me a political pornographer's eye for this land.

It is not only I who feel this regret and resentment – Robert's notion of 'pornography' brings together many feelings I have talked about with friends. I remember once, when I was walking with Jonathan, just walking in the hills, we suddenly found ourselves thinking like Israeli strategists – where we would establish a settlement if we were occupying this land. And that is how we have begun living – casting furtive looks at the settlements already there and thinking of all the other hills as prospective victims, pawns in a political battle.

We caught ourselves at it and were disgusted – we have become incapable of sustaining a normal walk in the hills. And Jonathan said, only half jokingly: 'Ssh, don't let them hear you. Must keep this secret.' He was only half joking because we who have lived a silent love for this land are left with the grim satisfaction of seeing that the Israelis will never know our hills as we do. They are already making endless, ignorant mistakes. For all their grand rhetoric, they are strangers. We samidīn may be turning into pornographers – but our love is not forgotten. The reason for our grief is also our strength – the secret of our sumūd.

The Visit

I was busy with clients yesterday morning when the telephone rang. It was Aharon from the nearby Gush Emunim settlement of Ofra. He wanted an appointment and I unthinkingly made one for this morning.

I had twenty-four hours to regret my busy-lawyer reflex.

The Ofra settlers are perhaps the most violent of the lot in this area. They have been the initiators of countless incidents of brutal intimidation. It could be a trap.

I spent the evening going over the possibilities and preparing my way out. It is difficult enough being a lawyer on the West Bank. I didn't need the complication of Ofra's attentions. Of course it could be a trick of one of our more zealous members – to see if I would collaborate with the enemy. But it was far more likely that Ofra really wanted something, and would turn nasty when I refused to go along.

To be honest, this morning I was quite excited. This would be my first face-to-face meeting with the creatures whom I had hated for thirteen-and-a-half years. I felt more than a twinge of curiosity as to what they were really like.

At 9 a.m., Aharon was let into the office. He had brought Boaz with him, also from Ofra. After exchanging handshakes, they sat down facing me across my desk. Aharon was to do most of the talking. His eyes did not focus properly – I kept on having to decide which one to hold. Boaz was fat, his eyes a weak blue. He leant back and smiled, rather stupidly I thought – no danger there. I concentrated on Aharon.

'What can I do for you?' I asked in English.

'We live in Ofra near Ramallah,' Aharon opened. 'Do you know Ofra?'

'Yes, I see it when I drive down to Jericho,' I answered in a neutral voice.

'Well, we in Ofra want to register a computer services company. We know several institutions in the area are beginning to turn to computers. Birzeit University already has one, and so has Bethlehem. We want to get into the business of selling them to you people. But first we want to register the company here and we want you to do it for us.'

'But why did you come to me, rather than to an Israeli lawyer?' I asked.

'It is our policy to use the professional skills of the locals. Our carpenters, builders, etc., are all Arabs from villages around us. When we told the manager of the El-Bireh Discount Bank that we needed a lawyer, he suggested you.'

'I am sorry,' I said, 'but I cannot help you.'

Aharon seemed taken aback, slightly insulted. 'But why not? You are a lawyer. This is a simple thing we are asking you to do.'

I answered very slowly and carefully, making sure to hold what I could of Aharon's gaze.

'I refuse because you are settlers in Ofra. I do work with Jews in Israel, and had you not been living on the West Bank I would have gladly offered you my help.' I made this clear because I had long ago learned that almost any criticism or refusal to collaborate was interpreted as anti-Semitism, and that as soon as that came in, things got nasty.

'But what difference does it make where we live?' Aharon answered quickly, with a rasp of annoyance.

'The difference is this,' I said in a measured tone. 'As far as I am concerned, Jewish settlements on the West Bank are illegal. It is not only my national identity, my being a Palestinian, that forbids me to work with you. It is on the basis of professional considerations that I find I am obliged to turn down your offer.'

'Oh, leave politics out of this. We have come to talk business,' Aharon answered, throwing a look at Boaz. His voice was abusive and impatient. And as I heard it I felt my reserves slipping. There it was again, the familiar and insolent suggestion that colonizing is merely business, nothing to do with politics.

But more personally infuriating was the implication that by refusing to do business with the colonizers, I was acting unprofessionally – in short I was nothing better than a 'primitive backward Arab'. I felt the blood rising to my head and I tried to regain control by starting on another tack.

'Let's drop politics for now,' I said. 'I have other reasons for refusing, as well. I am curious to know, from a strictly business point of view: once you have established your company, do you really think Palestinians on the West Bank will make use of it?'

'Why not? We live in Ofra, you live in Ramallah. We have expertise we can offer you, just as you have expertise to offer us. Why should any of the locals refuse to do business with us? We are bringing progress to the area. Do you want to say you're against that?'

His voice had become high-pitched and I could see that he was getting worked up. And still I couldn't stop myself. I just couldn't believe that he was serious.

'But surely it is not quite so simple. Most Palestinians feel as I do. They will not want to have anything to do with the settlers,' I said.

'But why? We are not depriving you of anything. The more settlements the more progress. How can that be bad for you?' Aharon retorted.

As he spoke, pictures of this progress flashed through my mind: rings of bright neon lights around Jewish settlements in dark Arab hills; sprinklers on Jewish lawns in the middle of dry Arab land.

'Do you honestly believe that it is so simple?' I asked, trying none too successfully to act the cool, collected lawyer. 'Your existence was made possible by taking the lands from Palestinians. You are allied with a military government that is persecuting us. To put it bluntly, you are the spearhead of the occupying enemy, determined to wipe us out.'

And here, at this stage, I was taken absolutely by surprise. Aharon's eyes lit up and he stretched both arms forward as if to embrace me and said in an excited voice: 'Ah – that is what you think! I see! But don't you understand? We, like you, have to fight the military establishment. They restrict our growth. Ofra was founded without the consent or cooperation of the military government. Some Israelis even dare call us "illegal". We came at night, set up our tents and for a long time lived in worse conditions than your people in refugee camps. I tell you – we were refugees. We have had to do everything on our own, fighting tooth and nail for it. We hate the establishment as much as you do.'

I was struck dumb for a moment. Is he deranged? Or is he

putting on an act – expecting me suddenly to realize that we have a common enemy and can work together against him? This was something completely new.

Stalling, I asked him what would happen when the military occupation ends, when we win the fight against our enemy.

Aharon was ready with an immediate answer. 'Why, of course, then we will all live in peace together in Eretz Israel.* We already have Arabs living in Israel you know. Look how well-off they are, compared with you before we came. We treat them well. Don't you see how good it will be – Arabs and Jews together in Eretz Israel? We all long for peace.'

Back to Square One – the manipulation of words – the history of our relations. I was to be the blood-thirsty Arab who refuses 'peace'. We had reached the end of our conversation as far as I was concerned. My curiosity, which had made me vulnerable, had run dry. I made a brief political statement about my determination to achieve a state of my own.

When he answered, Aharon's voice had also changed completely. He became hard and business-like, authoritative: 'Let us not get into that long story. We have settled here and are here to stay. That is a fact and there is nothing to talk about. Either you help us or you don't. I should remind you that you have no right to deny us your services. It is illegal.'

This was a definite crude threat, a reminder where power lay. I replied, equally coldly, that I had never heard of a law forcing a lawyer to work for anyone against his will.†

There was a tight, cold animosity in the air, and suddenly Boaz, who had not opened his mouth throughout the conversation so far, piped up: 'If you want a state why don't you go to Jordan?' His voice was jolly – he really sounded stupid. He

---

*Greater Israel, which includes the West Bank.

†N.B.: December 1981: I subsequently discovered that this was one of the military orders in the occupied territories that I had not managed to get hold of. Order 538 does in fact expressly make it a criminal act in the occupied territories to withhold one's services 'unreasonably'.

had obviously been told that Jordan was the Palestinian state, and was repeating his lesson.

This idiocy broke the tension; I could deal with him – and I told him why this was not a good idea. My parents had been forced to leave Jaffa in '48, I explained, and I saw no reason why we should be made refugees twice over for the sake of Greater Israel.

There was quite a long silence. The tension had been broken before we came to blows. Aharon got up and said: 'It is obvious that you don't want to do business with us.' I saw them to the door.

Postscript
In 1906, Ber Borochov, the Marxist, Zionist teacher of the establishers of the State of Israel, Yitzhak Ben-Zvi and David Ben-Gurion, wrote from his native Russia: 'Only laymen consider them [the residents of Palestine] as being Arabs or Turks. In reality, they have nothing in common with them. On the contrary, they think that by right the country belongs to the Jews. They will assimilate economically and culturally with those who will establish order in the country and develop its resources.' (Quoted in Amos Eilon, *The Israelis*, p. 60, Adam Publishers, Jerusalem, 1981.)

From the socialist visionaries who created Israel, to the right-wing fanatics who are stealing our land: it seems that – as far as dialogue, communication, minimal understanding between Jews and Palestinians are concerned – nothing has changed. Perhaps, for Israelis who want to draw moral distinctions between the first, socialist visionaries and the right-wing settlers of today, there is a difference – the difference between excusable ignorance on the part of people writing in Russia and the inexcusable ignorance of an Israeli today. But for us Palestinians who suffer either brand of blind denial of our full-fledged, independent existence, it has been the same story from the day it began.

The World Is Like a Wheel, Like a Cucumber

'The world is like a wheel,' my friend said, 'exposing different faces at different times.' He was talking to a group of Hebrew University professors who live in a high-rise apartment house on the French Hill in Jerusalem, near the university's Mount Scopus campus. The land had previously belonged to my friend. It was expropriated by the state for 'public purposes'. On what remains of his backyard, the Israel Land Development Company is now planning a parking lot for the university professors' cars. To do this, the level of the ground has to be raised, and the cars will be parked just under the windows of his children's rooms. He is to be left with his house only – with not an inch to spare or breathe in around him.

My friend has exhausted all state, municipal and other legal channels. The only thing left for him was to appeal to the humanity of his neighbours. 'We are neighbours now,' he told them. 'Would you like my children to curse you in their heart every night and every morning as they are awakened by the lights of your cars and the noise of their engines? Can you be sure that they will not grow up to be stronger than I and that they will not destroy you when they can?'

It was during this same visit that he expounded his belief in the inevitability of the fated change when the wheel turns. 'Now you can dictate your terms, take my land and park your cars under my children's windows, but it will be different when the wheel turns.'

As he told me of his talk to the professors, I could not help thinking that it must have had little impact on his intellectual listeners. My suspicion was confirmed when he told me of the answer made by one of them, who spoke Arabic. '*Ed-dinya zai lekhyara* [The world is like a cucumber].'*

---

*The unspoken ending of the saying is: '. . . one day in your hand, one day in your ass'.

My friend took this as agreement – a cruder way of expressing the same thought. He missed their condescending sarcasm. These professors will not be intimidated by fatalistic talk – science does not support it. They were just playing along with our 'primitive folk-mentality' when they laughed and produced their coarser saying.

It is true that a rigorous mind refuses to ascribe change and development to fate. Yet is it not possible that the children of my friend will grow up with wills stronger and more determined than those of the professors' children? My friend's children are being moulded by memories of lying on the ground, trying to stop with their bodies bulldozers which are tearing up their favourite trees in the garden. What experience have the pampered professors' children to harden *their* wills? I am sure that there is some scientific description of the change that will come. But I prefer my friend's wheel of fate: it helps me conceive more graphically of my sumūd.

The Wheel

Returning from the airport, where we had picked up my aunt, we were stopped just after midnight at the checkpoint where my mother and I had the tragi-farcical encounter with the soldier some months before. This time, I was sorry I didn't have the bag of earth. Lacking this additional diversion, the soldier – a different one – immediately ordered us to take off the wheels. I said to my uncle: 'Well, that's one talent I've picked up under occupation. Who said it doesn't benefit us?'

My uncle was not amused. My mother and my aunt were ordered, at gunpoint, to stand near the wall. My uncle was exhausted – his back is in bad shape – so I suggested that I do it alone.

'Get on with it – both of you.'

My aunt began pleading on her husband's behalf, and was ordered to shut up and not make a move.

Clumsily, my uncle and I unscrewed one wheel after another. Once they were all on the ground, the soldier said: 'Now put them on again.' I too was exhausted, and somehow it assumed for me a sort of ceremonial air; the ritual of humiliation. When we had finished, the soldier let us go.

We rode in silence until we got on to the Latrun road. Then we all sighed with relief . . . we were back in our own territory – the West Bank. Suddenly, as we were taking a turn, the glaring headlights of an army command-car reared up ahead of us – in our lane. My uncle barely managed to brake in time to avoid a collision. The driver, and some soldiers who were sitting in the back, jumped out of the car.

'Get out, get out, all of you!' the driver screamed into our car.

'Why?' my uncle asked in a reasonable voice.

'Why! Why, you ask – you idiot. You were going to make us collide with you. Get out!' and he made for the door handle.

We climbed out, with my mother apologizing: 'We're sorry, we're sorry – we didn't mean any harm.'

As I stared out into the velvety night I could barely hear or see what we were going through. It sounded far away – dreamlike. My mind was taken up with a vivid image of what had happened to my aunt's brother. In 1967, just after the war, he was driving with a friend back from Tel Aviv. Not far from where we were now, their car was stopped by some soldiers. The soldiers marched them off into a nearby field and shot them. Then they dipped the murdered men's kufiyehs in petrol and set their bodies on fire. Their remains were found, days later. The story was revealed by a local village woman who had seen it all. She testified at the soldiers' trial.

I don't remember what exactly went on that night. None of

us do. We were all enacting in our minds the night of my aunt's brother's death. Petrified and numb with fear – we cannot have been much fun for the soldiers. Perhaps my mother's sobbing reminded them of their own mothers. And we men seemed broken-spirited and useless. At some stage they ordered us into the car. One of them kicked me from behind as I stooped to get in. I barely noticed.

Thirteen years – and the wheel has not turned. Thirteen years – and the cucumber is still in their hand. The age when the wheel stands still is the age of my sumūd. When it turns – my sumūd can end. When will fate harden my heart enough for me to give that tiny push that will free the locked wheel?

Autumn 1980 Journal

October 14
Hebron Mayor Fahd Qawasmi and Halhul Mayor Muhammad Milhim have been allowed to return while their expulsion is reviewed by a military panel. They were expelled hours after the May 2 fedayeen attack in Hebron, just dumped across the border – against even military regulations which allow people to appeal against banishment before a military panel. It is because of the summary way they were expelled that the High Court has ordered a review.
 The hearings will be held at a makeshift court near the Allenby Bridge. If the expulsion is upheld, the mayors will appeal to the Israeli High Court of Justice. Father is going to prepare an affidavit on the illegality of the expulsion according to Jordanian constitution – which is still in force here, except where explicitly revoked. Another affidavit is being prepared on the Geneva Convention which prohibits any form of expulsion.
 There is wild hope amongst many because the thousands of expulsions by the military have never before been contested in the Israeli High Court. It has been assumed that this is within the untouchable control of the military. If this works, it will be an air-vent, an opening. Even the political die-hards who say we should never appeal to, or recognize, any Israeli institution are excited.

October 16
Today, about two weeks after the book* came out, I had a

---

*The West Bank and the Rule of Law.

telephone call from the adviser on Arab affairs to the military government. He said that they had considered banning the book, but decided against it because 'that would make you a national hero'. I thanked him for sparing me that fate, and waited for him to elaborate, but he did not; he said a tight goodbye and hung up.

I was sincere in my thanks, as far as they went. Our national heroes seem to be fated to spending their days entertaining streams of admirers and visitors with endless cups of coffee. But it is not only they who pass their nights in fear of the military. Any Sāmid can be picked up by a jeep, jailed, tortured and – my greatest fear now – banished. So the adviser's curt phone-call was not very informative, let alone reassuring.

The horrible fears of the summer are with me again. I wish they would make some definite move.

October 17

I am very worried about a case I am working on. My client is young, nineteen, and is to be tried in a military court for 'membership in an illegal organization'. He has clearly been severely tortured; during one of our meetings he had to be supported, and almost fainted.

And I know it will be absolutely impossible to prove it. His family are anxious that a big thing be made of the torture during the trial. They also want their son to get up in court and declare his undying faith in, and loyalty to, the cause, his pride in being a fida'i. They say that, unless I follow this line, they will hire another lawyer.

I usually manage to follow a middle course between two alternatives that I find equally wrong – but I am afraid that it won't work in this case. The first, which I find almost criminal, is the ideological line, followed by lawyers who put their party interests before those of their client – making capital for the cause of our political prisoners. They use the court as a platform for their views (some of which I happen to share), stamp about contesting the legality of the court, arrange interviews with journalists in which they denounce Israel as racist, imperialist, fascist, etc. In court, they dwell on tortures they can't prove and have their client stand up and declare his belief in a Free Palestine. He is ordered to be removed from the court for abusive conduct and sentenced to life imprisonment. Yelling 'Freedom, freedom' all the way, he is packed off to jail where he can contemplate the freedom he has lost, thanks to his lawyer. If he is famous enough, the lawyer will visit him once in a while in prison and talk about how wonderful it must be to be locked up in the cause of freedom.

It might seem obvious that if you believe, as I do, that a lawyer's first obligation is towards his client and not towards their (shared) political aspirations, you should insist on conducting the case in a way that will not antagonize the court and will perhaps secure a reduction in your client's sentence – that is what, as a lawyer, you are hired to do and are morally obliged to try to fulfil. But it is far from straightforward, for many reasons. With the parents of this client, as with many others here, I know that if I were to refuse to conduct the case unless they agree to my way, he would fall straight into the clutches of one of the ideologues who would be only too glad to build up the case for political reasons in a way that would ensure that the boy gets the maximum penalty.

But even if this weren't to happen, if there wasn't this danger, matters are not clear-cut. I find the radical alternative to the ideologue equally distasteful and wrong. There are lawyers who refuse to have anything to do with a client unless he is prepared to grovel – to denounce in court all his political and moral beliefs, to say he was misguided, threatened, confused, etc. He is made to apologize for, and renounce, everything he believes in and has fought for, and in return perhaps gets a reduction from the maximum penalty.

Apart from anything else, the reduction that this grovelling gains him is usually very small – five years off a thirty-year sentence. And his life in jail will be miserable – he will be treated as a traitor and a coward by all the other prisoners – humiliated on all sides and totally isolated. And finally, if the difference is so small, is it worth giving up every shred of self-respect you possess? I don't think this is right either, and I usually manage to work out some compromise that won't involve publicly renouncing everything my client has fought for, but will still minimize the court's antagonism.

But I am worried that nothing will work in this case – that the family is too convinced of what it wants, to allow me to conduct the case in my own way, and that they will shunt their son off on to a legal 'freedom fighter' who will salvage his own political conscience and ego by sending his client off in a blaze of rhetoric to the longest jail-term possible.

If only I were surer, more clear in my mind of what the boy's best interests are, on how to gamble on securing them, I would probably be more persuasive with the family. But time is running short – and he is so beaten and tortured. I must think clearly.

October 19
Enoch came to visit this afternoon to congratulate me on the book. I told him he was being premature – I'm not yet a national hero. 'Never mind, keep trying,' he laughed. We raced down Batn el-Hawa. The land is parched and brown as I love it best. We rested by a *qasir* (the round stone towers dotted all over the West Bank, used by olive-pickers to store olives and sleep on top of during the harvest). It is so easy to be transported centuries back as soon as you leave the town and go out into these stony hills. Enoch disappeared into the tower and emerged from its top. Silhouetted against the sky with his long beard flowing, he looked like one of his people's ancient prophets.

We talked seriously for a while. I told him about my crazy fears over the book – how I quail at the sight of an army jeep – how I wish something definite would happen. And I also confessed my wild hopes for it. Enoch said that I exaggerate both in my fears and in my hopes. 'Despite everything you know and say, you still believe that the Israeli public will be appalled when it reads about the machinery of legal oppression it has set up here. But the book will only be read by those who care anyway, and they are very few and very silent. The wise adviser on Arab affairs is no less an expert on Jewish ones. He knows that, as far as the Israeli public is concerned, there is no need to ban the book. You think the Israelis would be shattered by what you document there. But nothing can shatter them any more. Nothing. They won't even notice it. They are too far gone.'

As Enoch was speaking I knew that he was spelling out what deep down I feared more than anything, and I was shaken by the way I had managed to protect myself from this by imagining violent reactions to the book. It is this: that law, reason, words – everything I deal with – mean nothing; that I have refused fully to acknowledge this for fear of having to confront my own impotence.

The sun had set and the soft rounded hills had turned into black, shapeless monsters. Enoch was speaking in whispers about dreams he had had and plans he had made, and of how little of all that he had fulfilled. He tried to make things easier for me. He said that Jonathan and I should be very proud. 'You actually got something done. Most people here just succumb to the silent despair.' He also said that it is precisely because there still are a few people who care, that it is important the book was written. 'Even if we are a very small minority, we deserve some attention as well,' he laughed.

Being with him, his warmth so much more real than my phantom nightmares, put off for a while the dizzy hollowness I now feel. And for all Enoch's generous words, I am not proud.

As I sit here writing, hours later, I still can't control the fears, however irrational. And added to them now is a horrible suspicion that in some very wrong way I was writing for the legal establishment in Israel – seeking out their attention, like a delinquent son trying to catch the eyes of his elders.

Otherwise I would not be so dejected. The minority Enoch mentioned would be enough. Or is it simply thwarted megalomania that is getting me down – the deflation of our pathetic idea that our dry little book on the niceties of law would change the face of a firmly and deeply entrenched military, economic and political occupation?

October 20
Yesterday the military panel hearing Milhim's and Qawasmi's case recommended, as expected, upholding the expulsion. Today, as expected, the military governor accepted their recommendation. Their lawyer has applied for a temporary injunction with the High Court to prevent their expulsion until an appeal is heard. Father has begun working on the affidavit.

October 21
I went to a government office in Jerusalem today. Moshe was, as usual, very helpful. He is an Iraqi Jew, with a stern, gruff manner but a kind heart. Today he shielded me from the wrath of another worker there, Arieh, who stamps up and down the corridors like an Ahab, terrorizing everyone in sight: secretaries, the public, even his colleagues.

Arieh was seriously injured and has almost lost his hearing, he is all stitched up and scarred, has plastic surgery and a false leg – alive only because of the latest medical innovations.

I remember the first time I went there with Father. Arieh was polite and tried to be helpful. When we left I asked Father if Arieh was a victim of the Nazis. Father said: 'No, he was injured by the big bomb the fedayeen put in a fridge on Jaffa Street.'

And Moshe protects me from the wrath of this man who has been made into a monster by a bomb laid by one of my people's fedayeen. A man whose life has been made a misery, and who makes Moshe's life miserable as a result of these injuries.

I say to you Moshe, with deepest admiration and respect: '*Kol Hakavod Haveri* [I salute you, my friend (Hebrew)].'

October 25

Jonathan and I had our second official reaction to the book today. We went to submit a request for a client for a family reunion in one of the West Bank towns. When we were let into the office, we found the officer in charge, 'Itzik' as he likes to be known, surrounded by *mukhtars*. They were drinking coffee and gossiping. Itzik is learning fast – he'd better watch it, he is definitely beginning to *go local*. Others have gone even further. They have become such experts on local habits that they are beginning to lose their moorings. I have heard about one who has begun sleeping in his office – he is so busy being local he has no time to go home. His wife, I hear, wants a divorce. She probably doesn't like the attitude to women that her husband has soaked up from the people he is surrounded by. I don't blame her, those willing to sit about with the governors are not known for their honourable conduct towards their women.

Itzik looked up jovially when we entered and asked who we were and what we wanted. When we told him our names, his smile remained fixed but I detected an unpleasant hardening in his eyes.

'So you are the boys who wrote that book about us!' he said in a tone of 'boys-will-be-boys-but-I-forgive-you-for-your-naughtiness'.

I wasn't quite sure how to react, so I said 'Yes', and politely asked him if he had liked it.

This was obviously not the response expected of me, I realized as soon as the words were out of my mouth. The smile evaporated, he leant forward and out popped the mailed fist – the wrath of the disciplining father. 'Did I like it, he asks! He wants to know if I liked it! That book is pure rubbish, ignorant lies! That's what it is!' He was red with fury.

I didn't know what was coming next – is this when I get arrested, the beginning of the hero treatment?

For lack of ideas on how to act, I asked him what he didn't like in the book. I was stalling, trying to find out what was happening and was astounded when he said, 'You don't think

I actually bothered to read it, do you? I've got more important things to do with my time!'

Perhaps the look of sheer surprise on Jonathan's face and, I imagine, on my own embarrassed him. He began to splutter something about our sending him a copy and he would tell us what was wrong with the book. He seemed to be struggling back into the role of benevolent father, teacher. I said as politely as I could manage that I would send him a copy and told him the price. He seemed disconcerted and I realized that he had assumed we would offer to send him a free copy – after all, he was doing us a favour by reading it. I said nothing. I certainly didn't want to waste a copy on someone who seemed to know what was in it without having read it. After an uncomfortable silence, Itzik muttered something about paying on receipt, and more or less dismissed us – probably relieved to return to the *mukhtars*, where his patronage is taken in the correct spirit. I have grave doubts about the success of the application we submitted.

If even Itzik, who is not exactly top brass, had heard about the rubbishy book, the word must really be spreading. Perhaps the reaction will merely be to stymie every move we make – to turn down all our requests – one cannot move a step here without the approval of some military official.

I wish I knew what they are planning.

October 27

On the way back from Nablus I stopped to talk with an old man I have become friendly with. He has an olive grove of several dunums north of Ramallah. Today, I found him loading olives on to his donkey from the *qasir*.

The sky was clear and the air crisp and gentle as we stood talking near his donkey, our voices trailing off into the silent hills around us. He looked out contentedly on to his sloping olive terraces, which have been in his family for over a hundred years. We agreed that the one good thing this year was the bumper olive harvest, the best in six years. It has been *sanat kheyr*.

While we were talking, the silence was invaded by the rumbling of a far-off bulldozer. It came from the direction of what looked like beehives on the horizon. I saw a crane poised majestically in mid-air, elegantly framed against the pure blue sky, preparing with precision to swoop down and change the order of things. The land we were looking at had been confiscated from villagers in anticipation of the growth of the new Jewish settlement – Beit-El – ('The House of God', the Hebrew name for Baytin).

'When the bulldozers stop to rest I hear the land sighing,' my friend said. We stopped to listen for a few minutes and then he prodded his donkey and began slowly making his way up the fields. There is much to do, press the olives, sell the oil, it has been *sanat kheyr*.

November 1
The Israeli High Court began hearing Qawasmi's and Milhim's appeal. Yesterday, Father was told he had forty-eight hours to prepare the affidavit. He will try to challenge, for the first time, the legality of the Israelis' right to expel, which they base on article 122 of the British Defence (Emergency) Regulations, 1945. These allow the British High Commissioner (now the Israeli Minister of Defence), to expel any person from Palestine. Until now it was assumed that when Jordan took over the West Bank in 1948, the emergency regulations pertaining to all of Palestine were not repealed and could therefore be reactivated by Israel. But Father will argue that they were implicitly repealed – in general, and specifically with respect to expulsion – by section 9(1) of the 1952 Jordanian constitution which provides that no Jordanian national may be expelled from Jordan.

Qawasmi's wife, Yusra, has been sitting in the office all day and doing everything she can to help us, acting as courier to the lawyer in Jerusalem who is representing her husband in court, taking things to the typist, bringing us the books we need and encouraging us all through the rush.

When nothing is required of her, she sits quietly in the room, trying to be as unobtrusive as possible. It is hot in the office and the air is thick with cigarette smoke. I watch her as she patiently listens to the history of the repressive measures adopted, repealed and adapted by the various rulers over this land. What does Yusra think, as she sits here and watches the professionally optimistic faces of the lawyers?

While her husband has been in jail, on hunger strike, Yusra has gone from lawyer to lawyer, appealed to the High Court, written to Israelis of goodwill, spoke to ministers – done everything any mortal can do. What will become of her if she loses him – how will she tolerate life without him? But she will not pack up and leave – her husband would not want that. We are samidīn – and the children must finish their schooling; it would be terrible for them to leave. She must keep the home here.

She knows all of this, knows what she is up against and yet her eyes are full of hope as she sits here, runs errands, does everything she can. Does she believe that with this much effort being put into saving her husband – it must succeed? She sustains all of our hopes – she is a brave woman.

November 4

My neighbour Um Hani was frantic. She rushed to my door as soon as I got home yesterday evening. 'The police have come for Hani. He must report tomorrow at 8 o'clock at the police station.' She was sure that after the long months of being left alone with his wound, the military had finally decided to put Hani on trial – they often delay charges like this. Hani's leg is getting worse and Um Hani was beside herself with worry.

This morning I went with Hani and her to the station. The Israeli officer could not see us, we were asked to wait. An hour later, we were taken upstairs to the officer by the Arab policeman.

The officer had a letter. He read it out in Hebrew with the Arab policeman translating. 'The possibility that you were shot by an Israeli soldier has been investigated. Not enough evidence was found to incriminate anyone. You can appeal this decision within thirty days.'

Hani said afterwards that he was too shaken to feel relieved. His mother hugged him all the way down the stairs. He felt embarrassed.

I asked them if they were going to appeal. No, they said. Why make trouble for themselves? The military governor would call Hani if they pursued this. It is useless anyway.

But Um Hani felt uncomfortable. She said she knows that, if she does not pursue this case, they would feel they could carry on similar actions with impunity. She said: 'Farha's son was leaving the house of a friend last night at 8 o'clock, going home. He was stopped at the Manara. The soldiers in a jeep asked him for his ID. They asked him to which school he went. He said he was not going to school, he was working. They didn't believe him and beat him up and broke his ribs. Now he is in hospital. If Hani and he and others don't take action, the soldiers will keep on doing these things. I cried, when I saw the pictures on Israeli news of the schoolkid shot in the legs. It reminded me of Hani's agonies. But I cannot take any more. I cannot fight this occupation alone.'

November 8
Tomorrow the High Court will end its hearings, and the mayors will wait until it hands down its ruling. It will probably take several weeks. Of all the arguments produced by the State Attorney for upholding the expulsion, the one that horrified me most was that the expulsion is not in contravention of the Jordanian constitution because the latter forbids only expelling from Jordan, and the mayors were expelled from the West Bank, under Israeli rule, to the East Bank, under Jordanian rule, so they are still in Jordan, and it is not really expulsion.

Despite this, I have a strange feeling of confidence that it will work, that Yusra will be rewarded.

November 9
At the YMCA in East Jerusalem this evening, I talked to some American Arabs who have come to have a look at 'their country'. They were very young, very well-off, born in the USA and here in search of 'roots'. I lingered to watch the programme that had been laid on for them as an expression of these roots they yearned for: dabkeh in 'traditional dress' (I suppose it looks 'cute' to them), Palestinian songs and skits about a farmer who had lost his land.

The event reminded me of the few months I spent learning Hebrew in an Israeli Ulpan, in West Jerusalem. There I was given lectures on Israeli folklore, taught Israeli dances (e.g. the dabkeh – called 'Debka') – all laid on to encourage my American Jewish classmates to come here one day and make this their home. They too were interested in roots.

Are we then repeating an Arab version of Zionist tactics? Is my role supposed to be that of the fulfilled, rooted local? The public-relations stooge – like Avigail my Hebrew teacher in the Ulpan? She would come in every morning looking fresh, wearing a smile of fulfilment and wisdom and mystery. She sustained it all through the five-month course until everyone, I am sure, wanted to remain to participate in her secret of happiness. And she would actually say: 'Stay here – in a Jewish state – a state of your people – and you will be proud and happy.' (She would, on these occasions, studiously avoid the eyes of another Arab on the course and myself.) An Israeli friend told me that at an Ulpan somewhere in the south of Israel, where they have 'absorbed' some Vietnamese refugees – they stage exactly the same performance, the land of our forefathers, roots and all.

The visiting Americans talked to me in an ignorant, pampered and condescending tone – clearly expecting me to go through an Avigail act. My stomach turned as I spoke to them, and I thought of the hundreds of thousands of Palestinian refugees in Lebanon who would not need to be convinced of the significance of a rooted existence in order to come here and make this their home. They would give anything to be able to live here.

When we left, my friend Randa said that the embarrassingly simplistic dabkeh tunes, composed for the programme to the words of 'I shall remain', resembled the Israeli national anthem, and that all the jazzed-up folk songs sounded like Israeli marches. 'And I thought nastily to myself – no, you won't remain, and don't bother to,' she said.

But perhaps beggars can't be choosers and we are supposed to encourage everybody to come here, opting for quantity instead of quality. And this happy act is one of the burdens that samidīn should take on. Is this what is happening – the oppressed imitating the oppressor's worst manners – creating himself in the image of his master, the better to overthrow him?

November 11
As I drove up Chicken Street to our vegetable-market-turned-Ramallah-Court-of-First-Instance, I had a twinge of longing for our majestic courthouse in Jerusalem, which the Israelis in 1967 took for their own district court – after moving almost all our main civilian judicial institutions to this vegetable-market complex. I missed the sense of cool, forbidding awe and was already in a sour mood when I was told that the judge who was to hear my case was, as usual, late. I decided to sit in on another trial while waiting for him to turn up. It was a murder trial, and the defence had just called a woman to the stand.

The trial, as is often the case now, was being held in the judges' chambers rather than in the more forbidding courtroom. The judges prefer it this way – they feel more at home, cosy. As I watched the female witness take the stand, quivering, the setting took on the sinister aura of a cruel and primitive ritual. The judges, the accused and the lawyers all seemed to be in one league, leaning back in relaxed, dominating assurance – united in ugly enjoyment of the woman's fear.

The woman swears by the Qur'an that she is 'approximately

113

forty'. She is not sure – in fact, she looks in her late fifties. She is tall, with beautiful, hazel eyes and a finely chiselled nose. She is wearing a worn-out fallahi dress and plastic shoes. She is shivering, though it is warm. Her head is wrapped in a threadbare shawl with remnants of green and red embroidery. Her eyes are lowered and she looks as if she is trying to hide in her shawl from the men closing in on her in the stuffy room. Men no different from the men at whose mercy she lives in the desolate village of Dahiriyyeh, where she tremblingly told the court she lived.

As she answers the questions, it is clear that she has seen much more than she will tell. It is also clear that she was given strict orders on how to testify, and that she is petrified lest she say something wrong. No, she did not see who fired the shot, she whispers. Yes, the accused is of her *hamuleh* (extended family). I look across at him, at the blue, fearless, lawless eyes of the Hebronites, some of whom were the local descendants of the crusaders. He looks quite unperturbed by the trial and smiles smugly to himself as the woman whispers her answers to the defence attorney – he has nothing to fear from her. Or from anyone else in the courtroom, from the looks of it.

During the coffee-break in the chambers, the judges complain about their hard life. One is phoning private schools in Jerusalem, trying to place his children where 'they will at least learn English'. Everyone is eating, hummus plates pile up. Then one of the judges suddenly gets up, grips his huge stomach and declares that 'his intestine is loose'. I have horrible visions of an unhinged intestine struggling to break out. I don't think anyone knows quite what he means, but it sounds impressive and I am relieved that there is general agreement that he must go home immediately. By this time it is almost 12 o'clock. I ask about my judge. I am told that he didn't turn up yesterday because he was held up at a roadblock near Nablus. I wonder what held him up today.

November 13
Maher said to me today: 'My mother used to be a good mimic

– she would have us all rolling on the floor with laughter, but she doesn't do it any more. She says *"alba intafa* [the flame of her heart is extinguished]".'

The women have the hardest time with the occupation. Most of them must sit quietly at home and suffer the weight of their men's hurt pride as it comes down on to them. And this weight can be suffocating.

But I sometimes think that those few women who manage to survive this are the strongest of all samidīn and it is they who will finally lead the revolt. They have the least to lose and no ego to be pampered, hurt or played on by the Israeli rulers. You see them fearlessly head demonstrations and shout at soldiers at road-blocks. They have been used to brutal oppression by men from the day they were born, and the Israeli soldiers are not a new breed of animal to them.

Perhaps it is the slow, deep flames of those women who do survive that will keep our sumūd alight, for it is they who know the patience and perseverance we need. Their flame is used to very little oxygen – the men's harsh, bright fire is much weaker.

But on the way, many, many women – like Maher's mother, like the woman in court two days ago – are suffering more than any of us, as their air-vents are stopped, one by one.

November 15
This morning I went to the military government headquarters in Baytin, to the wing dealing with security and law. There sits the adviser on Arab affairs, studying the Arab mentality and mood, and advising on what measures should be taken to tighten the grip. Next to him sits the legislator and legal adviser to the military governor. It is to this 'one-man parliament' of ours that I went to inquire about Military Order 854 pertaining to universities and other institutions of higher education on the West Bank. It was issued in July and I have just heard about it.

Alex, who from his accent I judge to be an immigrant from England, was the officer I met today. He was extremely polite and helpful and took down the files containing the material I sought. 'We didn't do very much,' he said modestly. 'We simply amended a few existing Jordanian laws.'

He showed me the one-page order. He should not have been so modest. With a few strokes of the pen, the little amendment and a few additional unnumbered orders had achieved a lot. The orders extend Jordanian laws concerning elementary schools to universities. Universities must now obtain a yearly permit from the military and are subject to petty interferences in textbooks, curriculum and structure. They also prohibit anyone entering the West Bank from studying there or teaching there unless he or she gets a special permit from the military.

No, Alex should not have been so modest. His expertise in Jordanian law far exceeds, I should imagine, that of a good lawyer in Jordan. They have now extended to education the control which they already have over our courts, health, welfare, labour institutions and all other fields of civilian administration.

And I, the privileged lawyer, must be careful to maintain polite relations. It is not everybody who is allowed to see the military orders. I keep a deadpan face and ask Alex about his plans, health, etc. He tells me that he has only a few months left in the army. He has been working very long hours and is exhausted. He can't wait to leave and set up his own office in Tel Aviv.

Alex was kind enough to give me a few copies of the new regulations – again a great privilege. I thanked him, wished him well in civilian life, and left. Outside the building there was a garden with a collection of primitive tools of the natives, my people, whom these overworked officials have to rule: a hand-plough, a mule-driven olive press, a sieve – all arranged tastefully around an elegant water fountain. This is where the hard-working officers rest from their burden, under the pine trees, probably proud of their little collection – it is not everyone who can recognize quality, the real, authentic thing.

November 16

When I left court today, I was stopped by a lawyer I know vaguely. He drew me into a corner and said that today was his last free day before he begins serving a six-month prison term. He asked me to help him – he said he had only a few hours left. This was his story:

Several months ago he was engaged to contest the sale of 600 dunums of land in a nearby village to a subsidiary of the Jewish National Fund – for a private Jewish settlement. The fund's representatives had frightened an old woman into signing documents selling the land. In fact, she was not its owner, and the family owning the land was now contesting the legality of the sale. The lawyer told me that a week before the trial was due to begin, he had a telephone call from someone in the military government warning him to keep off the case. He refused, and a day before the trial he was arrested on suspicion of driving without a licence. The land trial began without him, and the claimants had to hire another lawyer at the last minute to replace him. He, in the meantime, was tried, convicted and sentenced to six months in prison and a fine of 7,500 Israeli pounds – an unheard-of penalty for such an offence – particularly as he was never stopped by a traffic policeman. He told me that he had asked for a week's deferment, so that he could settle his cases, transfer them to other lawyers, etc. Today, in another two hours, he would begin serving his term.

He was unhappy, he said, with the way his replacement was pursuing the land case. He believed that the military authorities had succeeded in intimidating the new lawyer – who was merely going through the motions of presenting his clients' case. He wanted to give me the relevant papers so that I could ask Father if he was willing to take up the case instead of him.

I was shattered by his story. And I was baffled by his attitude. He spoke without expression, matter-of-factly, as if this was all in a day's work. I couldn't understand how he displayed no signs of outrage and how he could face the prospect of six months in prison so coolly.

I went with him to his village to pick up the papers and, as I drove away, I saw a police van drive up to his door. His time was up.

On the way home, I stopped off to discuss the case with some friends. Some nodded their heads wisely – haven't you heard about him? He is a collaborator. The whole trial is a charade. Others were less sure, but thought there was much more to the story than he had told me.

Our talks were, of course, inconclusive. Some believe he is a hero, others say he is a traitor. The network of rumours spread by the authorities, I sometimes think, is their most effective weapon.

But one thing he told me haunts me more than anything else. He said that the Jewish National Fund was also represented by a West Bank lawyer. When he asked their representative why he had not taken an Israeli lawyer, the man had told him that that is part of their policy, to use us Arabs to transfer the land – let us do all the work so that it can never be said that the land was taken against our will.

One of our people at my friends' house this afternoon was a member of our gallant band of striking lawyers. They and the judges must hold a world record: a thirteen-and-a-half-year strike. He had the gall to say: 'All of you lawyers who work here are collaborators. Every move you make is used to consolidate the Israeli occupation.'

It is true that this is a nightmare that haunts those of us who didn't go on strike. But if the majority who did hadn't been so busy resting their conscience, keeping it unsullied, letting the takeover happen before their very eyes without moving a muscle – then the burden of our nightmares wouldn't be so heavy. It is their not being around to fight the Israelis that has let the military get away with so much, and our civilian courts fall into the shameful condition they are in – which is exactly how the Israelis want them.

I was too furious to answer him – partly because he hit where it hurts most. I find myself suddenly thinking of us lawyers here on the West Bank as the daylight equivalents of the people dragged out in the middle of the night to whitewash over the slogans painted on the wall. It is as if by our very willingness to function under the distorted rules of 'justice' that they have set up here we are providing the occupation – the theft of our land and liberties – with a clean bill of legalistic health.

Just as the layers of whitewash sometimes crack to reveal the smothered earlier cries of freedom of our people – if I am, unwittingly, a whitewasher – I pray that my whitewash, which I cannot see, will crack.

November 17
They are at it again.

This evening I saw them roaming the streets. Fully armed soldiers with rifles, ammunition, walkie-talkies and water bottles strapped to their belts. In groups of two and three they stalk this jungle of Ramallah full of dangerous enemies. Sometimes they get hungry and stop to buy pretzels and potato chips produced by Osem (an Israeli food company) and everybody in the shop freezes until they leave. Then they saunter out into the street again and accost anyone in a kufiyeh – the dangerous ones.

It started three days ago. The students of Birzeit put on a cultural week: an exhibition of Palestinian art, plays, fashion shows of Palestinian dress. The military governor rushed to Birzeit, saw the exhibition and ruled that expressions of Palestinian culture are dangerous political acts. He closed the university for a week and declared the town of Birzeit a closed area. All the students took to the streets to demonstrate against the closure. The area commander declared on the Israeli radio: 'We shoot at demonstrators and will shoot at anyone who disturbs the peace.'

Palestinian culture is still in the making. The direction it takes and the subjects it turns to are being determined by our oppressors. 'We did not drop from the sky,' a student answered an Israeli journalist who asked him if the commander wasn't justified in closing the exhibition, as many of the paintings were 'political'.

Out of lived experience, culture and folklore develop. Our ballad heroes now are those maimed and killed by Israeli soldiers. No matter how many more boys and girls will limp for Palestine, we will not forget who we are. You will just leave your scars on our faces and bodies, but they will remain Palestinian faces – and bodies. However many exhibitions you close down, and however many soldiers you send out against us, we will not forget who we are.

November 19
Driving Ruth back to West Jerusalem this evening, we were stopped by two Arab policemen near Manara Square. They asked for our IDs. I produced mine and it transpired that Ruth didn't have hers on her. One of the policemen said that he must take her to military headquarters for questioning. 'Jews must have IDs on them as well,' he said primly.

I agreed politely and said that it was a silly mistake on her part and that we were sorry, etc.

But he wouldn't let us go. 'We have orders to take in for questioning any Jewish woman seen with an Arab – whether she has an ID or not.' I was astounded and asked him what kind of orders – written? military orders? – what was he talking about? He became a bit incoherent – but it turns out that these are unofficial, standing orders, issued by the military to the local civilian police. We argued for a while, his friend was anyway inclined to treat it less seriously, and we were finally allowed to drive on – promising 'never to do it again'.

I have never come across this one before. No end to surprises. I must find out more about it.

November 22
It is horribly clear. I think I have finally figured out what the experts on our mentality have decided to do with Jonathan and me. We shall be given kid-glove treatment, be exceptions

to the rule – and all this to disprove, where they can, things we wrote in the book. This is what is happening more and more often with the military orders. One of the subjects we wrote about was the lack of access to the 860 or so orders that have been issued since the occupation began. And now I find myself getting appointments and being allowed to see various officers in the military legal adviser's department, all too anxious to give me the special privilege of seeing the orders – which should be public to everybody. But they are still finding it difficult to quite let them into my hands – this won't be an easy policy for them to follow.

Today, I met a Druse officer, a proud recruit to the military government. Smart uniform, spectacles – he is a student of Jordanian law – another of the military governor's advisers who say how the Jordanian constitution should be amended to suit the military's intentions.

I have been trying for ages to get hold of thirty orders missing from the collection we have managed to scrounge together in the office. Today, the Druse showed me Hebrew copies of the missing orders and I saw that, interestingly enough, all these orders had to do with establishing Jewish settlements in the West Bank. And no less interestingly – that these are the only orders that for some reason never got translated into Arabic.

When I asked the Druse for a copy of the orders, he said he couldn't give me one because the orders had not been translated into Arabic. So I said I would translate them myself, if he gave me a Hebrew copy. Then he said that he only had this one single copy of the thirty orders. So I suggested that I take this single copy of the thirty orders and photocopy them in the next room. He said he couldn't do that without asking his superior. So I said, 'Well, please ask your superior.' He said he couldn't because his superior had gone home. So we made a date for tomorrow. I wonder what will happen then.

He explained to me confidentially, unofficially as it were, that the reason the orders weren't available and hadn't been translated was that the Arabs don't care about law, don't understand it, don't bother to file the copies of the orders. I did not ask him if he was an exception to the slothful Arab because I have learnt since the occupation that the Druse in Israel aren't Arabs but (or so we are told) proud honorary Israelis.

It was the end of his work day. So I offered him a lift back to Ramallah. He said primly: 'No thank you. We are not allowed to accept lifts from residents of the *shtachim.*'* (This is one of the new categories of Arab to come into existence since the occupation. We are also referred to as 'the '67 Arabs' to distinguish us from 'the '48 Arabs' – those who remained in Israel. The latter are also called the 'inside Arabs' – as opposed to us 'outside Arabs'. Druse and '48 Arabs unite when the term applied is 'the minority sectors'.)

Yes, this is what is going to happen: special treatment . . . polite smiles. And it would be criminal not to use this hateful privilege to find out what the orders are about– there is a limit to the amount of nose one can cut off to spite one's own face – so we shall have to go along with this horrible charade – which I suppose is no worse than others we go through.

November 24
More students shot, I think the number is twelve, scores arrested, Birzeit University surrounded. The students have begun a strike against Military Order 854. Demonstrations spreading to other towns, schoolchildren too. Soldiers everywhere.

Fahd heard them knocking on his door late last night. He escaped from his bedroom window and climbed a tree, where he hid all night. They did not leave until early morning. He made it this time, but they will come again.

'Now we are driven into the trees,' Fahd said, 'and when they say, "We shot in the air and killed some students", they won't be lying. We shall no longer have to talk about "flying

---

*'Territories', in Hebrew – one of the terms used by the Israelis to refer to the land occupied after the 1967 War.

Palestinians" to explain how shots in the air manage to hit flesh and blood.'

November 25
It is strange. Today I had one of those moments of total recall and relived feelings from my childhood and teens that have waned during these years of sumūd. I walked out into the hills – away from the streets littered with the remains of burning tyres, the children running from soldiers, the shop-doors welded shut by the army – I walked out into the world of my childhood. I stood on the westernmost point of the Ramallah hills and heard again the voices of the grown-ups, like a recurring chant: 'We are here in Ramallah only for a while. We are camping here until the day we return to our lovely land. Soon our *ghurba* [exile] will end.' And they would stand with me where I stood today, and point out to the sea on the west and say: 'Our land is there, where the plains are green and the orchards abundant.' And this is how I grew up – thinking of our house as a campsite in hard, dry land. I would spend hours in the rocky hills with thistles around, looking out towards the blue, hazy, soft spot where the sea nestled. And I saved my love for that magic land, and at night Jaffa's lights filled my dreams. It did not matter that other lands were accessible. It was there that I wanted to be – here in rocky Ramallah I was only camping.

As I sat on a stone today looking west, I felt it all, vividly. And I tried to remember when it was that I realized I loved this rocky land, when I began to treat it as mine. I suddenly remembered seeing – very early on, when the occupation began – a group of Jewish schoolchildren near Ayn Kinya. A sign on a bus nearby said that the tour was organized by the American Zionist Youth Movement. Four older boys, about my age, guarded the pupils with submachine guns. I remember the hate, the hurt anger that I felt when I heard the instructor telling the boys that the olive trees they saw were the offspring of those planted by their patriarch Abraham, and that the terraces were built by the ancient Jews, who after years of wandering in the wilderness settled in the Promised Land. And then the instructor said in a harsh, nasal English that I can hear now: 'See how badly this land is treated. It cries for you – for its true beloved sons to tend it back to life. You will make it bloom again.'

And I remember now how I looked about at the land he was pointing at, at the hills I had quietly loved while my more romantic dreams were fastened on Jaffa; and thought: you treacherous hills, lying there so modest and silent. Soft and unassuming, you are a harlot, slyly seducing these boys. And I remember how, from then on, I grew increasingly jealous, possessive and angry at the same time. I finally began thinking of this land as seducing us all into war – calling us into its lap to fall bleeding – a vampire that will suck our blood as we fight for it. You, who were only a temporary camp for us – now we will die for you – you have pulled these boys here as Jaffa pulled them – again we shall die for our land.

I wondered at the beginning of the year when it was I learned the art of pornography. It was very early on. My language may have changed, but years later I feel exactly the same: this land is going to soak up our blood for generations to come – and I hate it for that.

Yet – for all that I loathe these hills for the blood we will shed for them – sometimes I look forward to the time when that will be my fate. For now, I must wait, be Sāmid, a lawyer – appear before the Objections Committee to object before a military court of my enemy about its piecemeal theft of our land. And I, the lawyer for my people, do not mention that the court is illegal, having usurped the right of our own civilian courts to deal with all land matters – there is no point in doing that if I am to appear before it. I do not mention that they have reversed the legal rules of evidence so that now, every one of my people who wants to hold on to his land must prove that it is his – instead of the usurpers proving that they have a right to it. Nor do I mention, except in learned articles, the extraordinary way this has come about: all our land which was once state land only in theory, has now been turned into the Jewish state's land in practice – its private property, to settle and build on as it sees fit. All of us samidīn have become illegal squatters on the land Israel claims for itself. Nor do I mention that the only way to prove legal ownership open to a Sāmid – tax records – has been deemed 'unreliable' by the Objections Committee – making a Sāmid's ownership almost unprovable.

No – I keep quiet about all of this in court, and revert to ingenious tricks, in the court's own tongue, to save a dunum here and a dunum there. I go on in my sumūd, prostituting my legal profession, myself, losing the land before my very eyes.

And so it happens that I sometimes long for the day I most dread – the day we samidīn will have to spill blood for this loved and hated land.

November 29
By 8.30, when I get to my office, the street battles are ended. The only reminders are the grimy remains of burning tyres and the weariness on the faces of the merchants in the main street.

Schools open at 7.30 a.m.; by 8.30, the pupils have carried out their resistance. The unlucky ones are taken to jail, beaten and abused. The others are sent home. And the merchants stand, confused between orders to close and orders to open, between the call of national duty, the thought of another day's lost profit if they remain closed, and the threats of reprisal from the military if they don't open.

If I had not heard from my friends in Birzeit what is happening, I would not be able to know it from looking at the street now. There stands Sami in his three-piece suit without a necktie, leaning in the doorway of his boutique, open for business as usual; and the men are sitting in the cafés playing dominoes and smoking nargilahs.

For all my sympathy for the students, I find it is the teachers I feel for most, up against all conceivable odds, pressured from all directions. They want the university open so that studies can continue. The authorities make this conditional on stifling any form of national and cultural expression. If they comply, the students rebel and go on strike, and they themselves give up any idea of academic independence for their institution. But if they don't, the authorities threaten them with closure and hold back on books and equipment they need.

Order 854 already severely restricts those teachers who are allowed to teach here. The academic standard they are desperately fighting to maintain will not only not rise; it is bound to fall drastically. Then the authorities will say: 'You are not a serious institution, just a "hotbed of nationalism", therefore we are closing your university.' How do the teachers strike a balance between the students, rightly angry and unafraid, as is the case with students all over the world, and the authorities who want the students repressed? The teachers' position encapsulates all that sumūd should be – building up our society from within – and all the almost impassable obstacles and pitfalls placed before it.

December 3
With so much happening to occupy my mind, I have managed not to dwell on my talk with Enoch about the book, and to shut off thoughts about the blanket of deathly silence that has greeted it. But, of course, this morning, when I did get my first reaction, I was terribly excited and nervous. I was asked to lunch with an Israeli law professor who has written quite scathing criticisms of the military legislation on the West Bank. I was invited together with a well-known international human rights figure.

When our host greeted us – I had as usual lost my way in Tel Aviv trying to find his home – he was very gruff and cold, and I thought it was because we were late. We sat down to lunch and suddenly, without any warning, he turned to me and began shouting a barrage of insults about the book – how dare I – I don't know what I'm talking about – he would not give me a first-year pass mark in law school, such ignorance, lies, distortion. I was, quite literally, struck dumb. With the Itziks of the world I expect it, can cope more or less – but here – I had thought among friends – I was quite without defences. I just sat in a state of shocked silence. My friend waited for me to speak up and defend the book myself. But I could not say a word.

This went on for what seemed like ages. Finally, as with Itzik, I asked what he didn't like – but here I really wanted an answer. I was hurt in a way no soldier could hurt me. But no answer was forthcoming. It turned out (and this I still cannot quite believe, I don't know what to make of it) it turned out, he *had not read it either*.

I do not remember what else was said at that meal. All I could hear was the banging inside my head.

Now, hours later, I can spell the noise into words; I can spell out what I have been too dishonest really to face: there is no one in Israel who will hear me. Not me, not the Arab. The Jews are the ones who may criticize or defend; they are the ones who may say – this is good, this is bad. On our behalf. And if they don't say it is bad, it isn't. And if you dare open your mouth – then the real hatred of you will spill out of theirs. And the contempt.

The bitterness I feel is directed at myself, not at them. How could I feel so hurt? After thirteen years . . . I thought I was so wise and cynical, so weathered a sāmid.

Where did I learn this convenient hope and trust in the 'other Israeli' that I have used to protect myself? I think it was at the very beginning of the occupation. I was taken by my family and introduced to Jewish figures they had known and admired in Palestine before '48 – for their liberality, humanity – the Western notions of democracy that they brought to the region. Somehow, it was the story of them that I chose to cherish – no matter what I said and saw. I thought: the good Israelis will bail us out as soon as they know what the bad Israelis are doing.

I put my trust in them like a child – and that is how I was, rightly, treated: someone to be spoken to, patted on the back, taught – but never heard. I have no one but myself to blame for the shock, the hurt. It was I who refused to believe that what I saw around me on the West Bank was quite real. It was I who would say 'I must be dreaming', it was I who would cling to an image of another Israeli far away from it all – an image that had absolutely no basis in the reality I saw around me.

I an no longer dreaming. Tomorrow the High Court will rule on Qawasmi and Milhim. We thought they would give us our rights on a silver platter. Everybody still has wild hopes for the ruling. But I know now how these hopes will be smothered. And it is all for the good. We will be freed of hope, and of dependence.

But what of Yusra Qawasmi? What will happen to her strong and gentle face? Her hopes? How can I say it is all for the good? How can I lose myself in such self-indulgent bitterness? Yusra is right to hope and she doesn't deserve the pain that will be hers tomorrow, for years to come. I wish there was something I could do to help her.

December 4
The Israeli High Court has decided to recommend not to repeal the mayors' expulsion.

All I can think of is their faces after these months of hope and work. They will be banished from their land – till when? From their wives, from their children – who will stay here and wait for them. For how long?

There were legal arguments of course, well-considered judgements. It turns out that Father's claim that the banishment was illegal – because the mandatory Emergency Regulations were implicitly annulled by Jordanian law – was already thought of in 1968 when the military government was establishing itself. In 1968, the Israeli military governor issued an 'interpretive proclamation' that said that all the British emergency regulations would be in force in the West Bank unless *explicitly* repealed by Jordanian law. The proclamation was issued 'in order to remove all doubt'.

As to Article 49 of the Geneva Convention – which imposes absolute prohibition on any deportation, mass or individual – this is what the court had to say: whether one interprets the prohibition to be limited to behaviour such as that of the Nazi practice of deportations for purposes of torture, or whether one interprets it 'more broadly' – it can be invoked only by states – not individuals; this is because it is part of *conventional* international law and not part of international *customary law*.

So stateless Palestinians can make no use of it – there is no law that will protect them from banishment. The court said as much – and referred the problem to politicians.

It all fits together – there is also nothing a lawyer can do. A lawyer is a useless Sāmid. There is nothing he can do to defend his fellow samidīn.

Faces, 1980

They did not tell me what it would be like to stay here and be Sāmid, my brothers outside. They could not have known. I shall tell them.

It is like being in a small room with your family. You have bolted the doors and all the windows to keep strangers out. But they come anyway – they just walk through your walls as if they weren't there. They say they like your room. They bring their families and their friends. They like the furniture, the food, the garden. You shrink into a corner, pretending they aren't there, tending to your housework, being a rebellious son, a strict father or an anxious mother – crawling about as if everything was normal, as if your room was yours for ever.

Your family's faces are growing pale, withdrawn – an ugly grey, as the air in their corner becomes exhausted. The strangers have fresh air, they come and go at will – their cheeks are pink, their voices loud and vibrant. But you cling to your corner, you never leave it, afraid that, if you do, you will not be allowed back.

Yes, I know what it is to be Sāmid – I can see it engraved on the faces of everyone around me.

I should perhaps have been warned by the faces of the earlier generation of victims, my older brothers in sumūd, who stayed in Palestine after the war of '48. But I could not believe it would ever happen to me. 'You are on a honeymoon now,' they said a bit sadistically when we met after the occupation began in 1967. I didn't, of course, listen to them. They probably said this because they hated the glow of assurance on my face – after all, I would say to them, this is a temporary affair, Israel can't rule over one and a half million Arabs. And America is sending peace envoys, and Europe and the UN...

Then, at the beginning, I still had an outsider's face. I remember how before '67 we used to wait for the 'insiders' at Christmas at the Mandelbaum Gate. Some years they came, other years we waited in vain – receiving no explanation. Next year they would tell us that they had been refused a permit to cross, the year before. And when we asked why, they said: 'We were not in favour with the authorities.' What weaklings we thought they were. We could not forgive them for looking so beaten, so exhausted, so lifeless. When we asked them what it was like in Israel, they would begin to speak, then would soon come to a halt. They could not express what they felt; we could not understand.

Now the roles have changed. Mandelbaum Gate has gone. The points of humiliation now for many thousands are the Allenby and Damieh bridges over the Jordan River. And if we failed to understand before, we have had the chance to catch up. Our visitors now come across from Amman, and it is they who ask embarrassing questions. Now we are colonized, our primary struggle is for survival. On our faces are the lines, the deep lines of adjusting to living under masters. We are the new insiders.

The servile expression on the face of Abu Abdu – one of the first to serve our new masters at the courts – has now become set as in plaster – a death-mask. He used to be able to shake it off when his master wasn't around. Today, when he answered me in the harsh, derisive tone of his Israeli superior, I understood why I have been seeing the Israelis less often. Abu Abdu can now take care of the business of oppression just as efficiently. His face shows it. It is masked for good.

The businessman, my client, looks euphoric at the bank, his face flushed with unexpected success, exceeding his wildest pre-occupation dreams, his pockets bloated with the money he is now making.

The eighteen-year-old – his eyes staring from a face moulded by the harshness of despair into that of an old, broken man. A cruel, humourless, beaten mask.

Most of us samidīn move silently – the bouncing, money-making collaborators are few. We slink about surveying familiar places we feel are no longer ours, remembering lives we can no longer believe in. We stand by the ruins, as our poetry-reciting ancestors were fond of doing, but we are mute. Mute like the many Muslim sisters you now see everywhere. Women are taking the garb of silence. It envelops their bodies as they move inside it with resignation. They have chosen solitude and repentance for sins they never committed, hoping this will save us.

And the children, the faces of the children. The streets are full of them – learning the ways of the occupied world, watching shopkeepers standing all day outside their shops, chewing watermelon seeds and puffing smoke in the air – bored, desperate, workless. They and the children watch apathetically as an Israeli truck creeps through the streets, distributing Israeli foods unobtrusively, quietly colonizing us.

All the distortions of occupation are etched into our faces: the creases of humiliation, frustration, resignation, despondency, lost pride, and greed, sinking deeper and deeper.

Our brothers outside cannot bear to see our real faces; they like to think of us as victorious, saved from it all by *Amwal es-sumūd* they ship to us from across the bridge. But neither the money, nor the beating of the drums of false victories, nor the glorious receptions we see on Jordan television for the summit meeting of the Arab heads of state and kings, can change our faces.

Will all these marks disappear with the end of the occupation, or are we branded for ever?

And what of my own face? They say it has become gloomy.

Charles described me as 'burned out'. Last night I dreamed.

> The telephone was ringing. It was a client who wanted advice, but I put him off, saying I didn't know enough about the matter. I closed the office and walked down into the street. There I saw a man sitting up straight in a barrel. He had cut out half his skull and was pressing stones into the hole in his head. Filling it with gravel. I and the others watched him. We knew he would die soon, but we watched him torture himself, drawing it out. Then, further up the street, there were other people sitting up straight, dying slowly. They were strikers killing themselves for the cause. I felt sadness as I watched their suffering, but moved on. Then I felt myself devouring earth. I scooped up handfuls and pressed them into my mouth. Then I thought I was spitting it out, but I wasn't. I was afraid that I wasn't. I asked the others: 'Am I spitting it out or am I swallowing it?' If I swallowed it all I would be dead – filled up with soil. But I couldn't stop. I scooped in more and more, devouring it ravenously.

Can this be true? I see suffering and brush it aside? I go on with my irrelevant work in the middle of a life-and-death situation and then I punish myself by committing slow suicide – filling myself with earth to return to it in death?

Life and death are on my mind. I do not understand it, I do not accept it. My grandmother died recently. Her death made me see how we are human, though some act as if they were not. She was too proud to be human. This made her suffering more difficult for her, and for us. I also learned that it is more difficult to love than to hate. I am not strong enough to love. I find it easier to be angry and to hate. The same goes for the Jews. I cannot get over my hate, and I know I am the worst sufferer in the end for that.

A few nights ago I dreamed that a man (whom I seemed to be defending in court) was condemned to death, and that I was participating in his execution. He was being tied and placed in a box and I was unconcerned and helped in tying him up.

Collaboration. That is what haunts me now. Today I had a meeting with a client who has been under lock-up for a long time. An Arab, whose job it is to interrogate non-security prisoners, brought my client into the room where I was sitting with the prosecutor and others. The prosecutor and the interrogator shook hands very warmly and asked each other how work was going. Then the interrogator pulled out a pack of Israeli 'Time' cigarettes and offered them to everybody present except my client. His gun was conspicuously tucked into his tight trousers pocket, over his packet of 'Time'. He had a strong body and muscular hands. His isn't an easy job. True, he is well paid and well treated, but he earns it. Some prisoners are harder to break than others. Some are so stubborn that he has to beat them very hard. So much so that he was reprimanded by his Israeli superior – there are strict instructions about these matters – no marks must be left. But he cannot always control his hands, although he tries. He respects his superior very much. Since the occupation his life has become so much better – he has been taught 'self-respect' – and how to shoot. He takes his gun home with him. He can speak Hebrew and is sometimes sent on training courses in Israel. He is a made man.

I objected about the state of health of my client. He didn't dare complain but it was obvious how badly beaten he was. The prosecutor went on speaking, making his statement. The Arab interrogator served us all with coffee. His eyes met mine as he stooped to serve – 'Aren't we officers of the law all collaborating in a common purpose?' they seemed to say.

Are we, are we, are we?

I feel empty: in the hollow centre of a wheel with rusty spokes. At the end of every spoke is a head – a haunted, hunted, greedy, cruel death-mask. The wheel begins to spin and I get dizzy trying to find my face among the masks. I look out into the other side, the backs of the masks, and instead of hollows I see twin masks – the fragmented faces of our occupiers: riveted to the backs of ours in a way that ensures that *we will never see each other*, as the wheel spins faster and faster.

I see many Israeli faces fly by. But three stand out – freeze the wheel for a moment of sheer horror. First, the slightly pudgy, bespectacled face of the Ashkenazi intellectual; around him his Sephardi and Druse imitators. They look at me with the arrogance of colonizers. Their eyes express surprise mingled with anger that I, the native, should dare to think that I understand what they are up to. Then comes the gross, almost unlined face of Ariel Sharon and his gang of thugs: a petrifying combination of retardation and power: they mean evil and will succeed. Their faces are blank, completely free of even a twinge of conscience. And last, and in some way more disturbing than any: the weak face of the 'beautiful Israeli' who is upset by the occupation, not because it is evil, but because it ruins his looks. And he has every right to be concerned, because the lines on his face *are* ugly: those of a pampered narcissist who sees in his ever-present mirror his beauty fading – and begins to pout.

The Israeli sides of the masks are, in general, pinker, plumper, more self-satisfied. But that is because they do not, cannot, see the backs of their heads. They do not know we are glued together on the same spokes of a wheel that is spinning us all to death.

Epilogue, January 1982

As I was driving back into Ramallah with Jonathan this afternoon, we saw a jeep draw up near some boys who were playing football against a wall in old Ramallah. A few days earlier a schoolboy had been shot in the hand by a soldier driving by the same place. Our hearts sank as we saw a young soldier jump out of the jeep. The boys began to run – the ball was in mid-air. The soldier caught it, kicked it back at the fleeing boys who, after a split second of amazement, laughed, caught it and kicked it back at the soldier. We left them all playing football, laughing, shouting. I feel myself smiling as I sit here in my room with the picture of the soldier-boy and the Arab boys suspended for a moment of peace in the soft twilight.

Jonathan and I were returning from a visit to Sabri, an old villager who is fighting the expropriation of one hundred dunums of his land for a Jewish settlement. The saga and the legal battle have been going on for more than a year. Every time we visit Sabri or he comes to our office, he launches into a long tale – the latest instalment in his single-handed fight against the army and the settlers. His deep-set eyes and sun-seamed face take on a multitude of roles as he enacts the drama. Today he told an officer who is supervising the tearing up of vines in one of the last dunums left to him: 'Why do you shoot in the air? Shoot at me, at my children. Until you kill us all, you will never get rid of us.'

And his face, the high cheekbones and gentle but stubborn eyes, make me proud. And sad. He means it. And one day the soldier-boy laughing in the twilight game of football will find himself pressing a trigger at a Sabri. For so much is clear now. Israeli soldiers, from frightened, innocent boys to unthinking tools of oppression, will very soon find themselves aiming their guns at a million-and-a-half samidīn – if the Israeli government persists in the policy it is pursuing. (They say that one of the soldiers who took part in the recent demolition of three houses in Beit Sahour cried afterwards and said that, when he had tried to object, his commander told him: 'You are a soldier. Obey orders and get it over with. We have more houses to demolish.')

I said that Sabri is fighting the Israeli army and settlers single-handedly. This is not quite accurate. Besides God, whom Sabri believes is on his side, Arab and Israeli lawyers are fighting his case with patience, determination and skill. Even if the war is openly declared, the battle-lines are not quite drawn yet.

A year has gone by since I stopped writing – since the despair of the death-masks. I have survived the despair, as others survive theirs, perhaps wiser, but certainly stronger in my determination to persist in my sumūd. Just as the Israeli government appears to be more set than ever on emptying the West Bank of us samidīn. It is objective fear of the tragedy which lies in store for all of us that I now feel, rather than personal fears in the present. As to the present, I can again see what I lost sight of last year – the individual faces on the death wheel, Palestinian and Israeli, who are struggling to stop its spin.

Sometimes I feel that it is the Israeli faces among them which are the saddest. There are worse things than physical oppression and hardship, and there is a sense in which we samidīn are lucky in that we have a definite enemy and clear objectives – a society to build. We have enough concrete day-to-day difficulties and dangers to overcome to keep our minds from the threat of the future. And sometimes I find myself wishing my Israeli friends had this simplicity.

I wrote last year of the 'third way', and of the daily living being the test of sumūd. It is a test I failed, perhaps because I didn't have the kind of hope necessary for sustaining a constant struggle. It is not hope for this or that to happen, nor hope for the far-off future. It is the kind of general hope you draw from people around you whom you love. It is the faces, on the West Bank and in Israel, that I love, admire, am proud to know, that have pushed aside my nightmare visions. And it is the strength of their humanity that makes me sure that it is not mere sentimentality to linger for a moment over the football truce between the Arab boys and soldier-boy. Our struggle is not senseless: it is not yet proven that good never wins the day.

Samed